Seeds Beneath the Snow

SEEDS BENEATH THE SNOW

Vignettes from the South

Arthenia J. Bates

HOWARD UNIVERSITY PRESS, WASHINGTON, D.C. 1975

Printed in the United States of America.

All photographs courtesy of the Library of Congress.

Library of Congress Cataloging in Publication Data

Bates, Arthenia J 1920-
  Seeds beneath the snow.

    CONTENTS: Silas.—Little Jake.—Runetta.—The shadow between them. —Return of the spouse. [etc.]
    I. Title.
PZ4.B3283Se [PS3552.A827] 813!.5'4 69-18851
ISBN 0-88258-046-9

In memory of my father, Calvin Shephard Jackson
my aunt, Mary White
and the late President of Morris College, Dr. O. R. Reuben
to
My sisters: Victoria, Susan and Catherine
My brothers: Calvin, Graydon and Leon
but
especially to my brother Edward Glenn Jackson, Sr.,
and his cohorts

Contents

Between the finite limitations of the five senses
and the endless yearnings of man for the beyond
the people hold to the humdrum bidding of
work and food
while reaching out when it comes their way
for lights beyond the prison of the five senses
for keepsakes lasting beyond any hunger or
death.

—*Carl Sandburg*
from "The People Yes"

Seeds Beneath the Snow

Silas

"Boy, come on in this line behind me. You don't have a drop of your pa's blood in your body, nor an ounce in your bones. Come on here."

The Reverend John Gallaway put his pistol away as Silas stood behind him.

"If you don't try to be a man now, Si, you never will."

"Yas-suh."

A deep sadness gripped the boy.

As far as he could remember, somebody had always felt the need to prod him. His mother urged him gently, his sisters and brothers rebuked him for his lack of courage; the teachers at school lectured him and the ones at church advised him. They all wanted him to become a man, but he had no exact image of what they wanted him to be within his view.

Through fifteen years of life he had accepted his lot. He expected to be mimicked and nicknamed. He never told his Sunday School teacher, Mrs. Sadie Watkins, that Little Jake thumped him on the head when she was not looking, and asked each time: "Is the watermelon ripe?"

Towering above the other fifth-graders, since he was fifteen, he had learned to accept taunts to the point of joining in the laughter at himself. He was robbed of all identity except that of being Samuel Jones' boy.

His father was the live wire in Dubose Crossing. He was an ordained dissenter. But more than all, he was absolute ruler of his household. It was his conclusion that a boy could best become a man by exercising his muscles. If he had a will of his own, the development of mind would take care of itself. Pampering and coddling a boy made him, according to his philosophy, "breath and breeches." He was the youngest man on his job; he had more children than any man on the job; he had less physical weight than any man on the job; but he could beat the last

one of them laying crossties. Now that Silas had reached man-
hood in terms of weight and physical stature, Samuel made
arrangements to hasten his full maturity.

Silas had hopes of passing out of the fifth grade for the first
time in three years, yet his father forced him to leave school in
the month of March. At that time Mr. Bossie Woods needed
more hands at the sawmill who would work for what he could
pay. The employees could not ultimately lose because he owned
the commissary which handled everything from shoe strings
to coffins. Wages or no wages, Mr. Bossie Woods was a good
man to know.

On a March morning, as the world of the South stood changing
her dark winter garb to a gala dress of green, Samuel Jones
called his son in to give him a word of advice. He hoped to lift
his son from childhood's garden to the world of men.

"Silas," he said to his son, "I've been carrying the burden of
this house now for a long time. You might as well start learning
about life while you're in my house, so I can give you a push
now and then. I didn't have nobody but Grandma to do that
for me. Mostly I had to make myself."

"Yas-suh."

"Suppose somebody had to push me to take care of your ma
and eleven head of children?"

"I dunno, suh."

"I help put myself in school, worked, served the church,
helped Grandma —"

"Yas-suh."

"Boy, hold your head up: Just forget about that schoolhouse
and help make yourself a man while I can help you."

"Yas-suh."

"You know Mr. Bossie Woods?"

"No-suh."

"Well, he needs some more hands. You can go in the woods, haul logs, or anything Mr. Bossie tells you to do. And you act like a man. You won't be helping me so much as yourself."

"Yas-suh."

"I'll take you over there Monday morning."

When Silas and his father reached the commissary, Mr. Woods "sized him up" immediately as the type of boy that the men would despise. They would consider him as the cause for ill luck in the woods as quickly as the appearance of a woman.

He knew that Macey Bone and Spurgean Rivers, the two men who knew the sawmill and owned the other Negroes on the job, would laugh him to scorn for sending such a joker as Silas Jones to the woods.

"Fine fellow you got here, Sam. Fine fellow. Good you startin' him to work before he gits to be a shyster," he told the father.

"No-sirree. He's going to be a man, a real man," Samuel bragged.

"Awright, Sam, I gotcha word now on your boy, so you ken betcha life I'm for gittin him goin. Just leave 'm to me."

"I'll say good day then, Mr. Bossie."

"Awright, Sam."

"Now, boy, you know well's I do you ain't got no bizness in them woods with th' other boys. They drink hard likker and cuss like the debbil, but they keep things rollin."

"Yas-suh."

"What ken you do?"

"Whatcha want, suh."

"Awright."

"Your ma learnt you to sweep?"

"Some."

"Well, you goin' to clean up. The rats cut up stuff, 'n I got traps down, 'n all like that. You go 'long and fetch some kindling and light a little blaze to git the air off the shop and then sweep."

"Yas-suh."

What a fool, what a damn black fool that Sam is, to think he's goin' ta make a man out this scary boy, Mr. Bossie thought.

Bossie Woods put a neat plug of Brown Mule tobacco in his mouth and began preparing paper sacks of sugar, meal and flour ranging from one to twelve pounds in weight.

When the neighbors discovered that Silas had a man's job, they inquired as to how he fared. He had heard the men complaining about their backs so he answered: "I'm mekkin' it fine 'cept my back," to keep them from knowing that he was doing soft work.

Silas Jones added years to his life at random during his first two weeks on the job. He was seventeen by the end of the first week, and twenty by the end of the second.

He knew within himself that he was nothing. The men did not tease him. They passed glances that were not scornful enough to make him feel anything at all. They did not force him to drink hard liquor. They did not even call him Samuel Jones' boy.

Silas' new maturity served him well until he filed in line at the commissary for his check. It did not matter so much that he had not done "man's work"; he would get money for his work.

As he neared the door he visualized how he would count the greenbacks out to his father. He did not know how much money he would receive, since his father had talked with Mr. Bossie, but it would be money that he had earned all by himself.

Macey Bone brought Silas back to earth. He was tugging the boy's sleeve, saying nothing. When Silas refused to speak or to move, Macey shoved him to the ground.

Silas tried to remember what his father had said about the way a man should handle a bully. And he knew that Macey Bone was a real bully. The Policemen of Randle Town never pursued Macey as far as Trigger Gap, where he lived behind the canning factory. The preacher at the Mission had said something about turning the other cheek, but Macey Bone had not really slapped him.

Most of the men were so anxious to get their pay that they ignored the incident altogether.

The Reverend John Gallaway (he never had a church of his own), who stood just ahead of Silas, felt obligated to help the boy, who cowered — with big teardrops rolling to the ground.

"Brother Bone," the preacher said gently, "you shouldn't bother that boy."

"Is that little black bastard yourn? If he ain't, you'd better sorta count your words."

"No. He bet' not be mine." The preacher raised his voice. "'Cause if he hadda, you'd a never took his place with me standing here."

"Look, preacher, save your words for Sunday, 'cause this ain't none of your damn rotten gut bizness nohow. That rotten bastard's bawlin' his liver out 'cause you dippin'."

"I see you're a man who won't reason."

"Reason my ass! I ain't lis'nin' to no sermon in a payin' line. If you got so much time, why don't you go marry your Sat'y-night whore?"

"Look here, man. I carry the Word of God, so I'll not have you slandering my name. You leave my business out this. I do carry the word."

"You ain't nothin' but a yard-ax preacher noway, Reb. You ever heard of a bushwacker what jest hit at the Gospel?"

"It's the gospel truth that I'll spill your filthy black brains right on this ground if you say another word."

Silas stood up and away from the line. He was afraid to move back to his place until the preacher encouraged him outright.

Macey rolled his bloodshot eyes at the preacher as he moved away.

Macey was angry to the point of bursting but he said nothing. He moved away from the line as if he were leaving. When the Reverend Gallaway reached the door, a brick struck his left temple.

The preacher fell.

When Bossie Woods came to the door to see what had happened, Macey was out of sight.

When Silas reached home, he forgot to count the greenbacks out to his father. He told him hastily about the incident.

"Boy," Samuel Jones said in disgust, "don't you know that a man won't cry? You got those two men to fighting just because you cried."

"But Pa, Macey Bone took my place."

"Look, Si, you're in a man's world, so you got to act like a man. Do you see me crying? Well, I bet not see you crying or hear tell of you crying. You're my son, and you might as well make up your mind to be a man whether you like it or not. You hear me?"

"Yas-suh."

So men never cried. At last Silas knew that men were people who didn't cry.

Silas thought about this great truth of life and realized that his father was right. He had attended funerals at the Mission for several years, but he could not remember having seen a single man shedding tears. The women yelled and jumped up from their seats, but the men sat still with bowed heads.

He resolved to be a man. He would not cry — not ever again in his lifetime.

When he attended the Reverend Gallaway's funeral, he wanted

to run to his mother and fill her lap with tears. He wanted to throw his body on the good man's coffin and say, "I caused you to die," but he knew that everyone would say, "Si isn't a man."

He dropped his head like the other men.

Little Jake

Mrs. Sadie Watkins was the kind of woman who seemingly worked for a laudatory obituary. And on knowing her and watching her perform each act of love for Little Jake, one could never doubt that a smile might somehow warm even her still form after death whenever the words were read:

> She leaves to mourn her loss, one son, Doctor (or Reverend or Attorney or Professor) Jacob B. Watkins, Jr., four (or five or six or eight) devoted grandchildren, and a host of relatives and friends.

Having waited so long for this one baby, Mrs. Sadie dedicated her life to training him the way that the Lord would have him to go. She kept Little Jake sparkling clean; she ironed every diaper which touched his bottom. Some of the other colored ladies tore up old sheets or bleached flour sacks or meal sacks to make baby breeches, but she used only Bird's Eye diapers, keeping them as snowy as Mr. Monegan's best white shirts.

When most of the babies began walking, they moved into the family circle — eating grits and gravy, peas and rice, beans and cornbread, or any other food that the others fared on. The typical mother manifested great pride in answer to the query "Hey, what you been feeding your baby with?"

"Woman, that boy eats what I eats. At that, he comes nigh eating up a house and a home."

Mrs. Katie Hunt, whose husband ran a neighborhood grocery store, accused her baby boy in a more selective manner:

"Why, that Lloyd of mine has eaten up the profit his daddy made and bit a great big hole in the principle."

If Mrs. Sadie gave her Jake grits, it was with a pat of butter and a soft scrambled egg. Sometimes she would save the drumsticks from the chicken and stew them to a frizzle so that with a little thickening it made a different dish for her little boy. And while the other children nibbled away on dry biscuits or left-over corn cakes, Jacob had light bread with butter and jam, an apple, an orange or a banana.

Some of the women in Dubose Crossing, who boasted about their use of the flour and meal sacks for diapers, also expressed their pride in making shirts for their little boys, slips for their little girls, pillowcases, dish towels, and even sheets out of them. She never put sack clothes on her Jake or used sack linen on his bed. She gave her sacks to an aunt in the country to make quilt linings.

To Mrs. Sadie, the church would be her first ally in helping to make her Jake a somebody. It was her first ambition to see her boy shine at the Mission, the community Baptist church. It wasn't the greatest church on earth, but it was large enough to inherit all of the pseudo-reverence of the big churches, their tendency toward heirachism and their predilection for guile. Being president of the Pastor's Aid Club, treasurer of the Missionary Society, a member of the senior choir, a teacher in the BYPU and the Sunday School, the unappointed co-ordinator of everybody's program and all community affairs, Mrs. Sadie set the stage for Little Jake's greatness.

He made his debut to Mission rites the Easter he turned three. He was too afraid to attend the practice sessions with the other children, so Mrs. Sadie trained him at home. On the night of the program she walked up to the table and demanded the mistress of ceremony to place Master Jacob Benjamin Watkins' name on the program for a solo.

"But Mrs. Sadie, he didn't practice here at the Mission, and the Superintendent said none of the children who didn't practice could participate." Eva Mae Jones rushed through her rehearsed opposition.

Mrs. Sadie almost lost her temper, but decided instead to be cooperative.

"I tell you what, honey — just put Jake's name first on the program, and that won't interfere with nothing you planned."

"But Mrs. Sadie —"

"Come here, Jake. Let him sit right here on the front, so that he won't be scared to go up. I'll sit here to take him up."

"Mrs. Sadie," — the younger woman began to sense her helplessness — "nobody but the angels suppose' to sit on the front row."

"Eva Mae, I taught you in the Primer Bible Class, and you ought not to go contrary here on me, and the program is about to begin."

Eva Mae looked up, pleading with Mrs. Sadie without speaking.

"Come on, Jake." She planked the scared child on the front row and sat herself beside him, blocking four little angels from their rightful haven.

The news of the little three-year-old boy who sang a solo for Easter spread through Randle Town like the fire in old Chicago. This response took Mrs. Sadie to the Reverend Jonas Simmons, the pastor of Shiloh, the First Baptist Church (Colored). The Reverend Simmons, editor of the Randle *Spotlight,* the voice of the little Baptist world, was also the recipient of plentiful gifts from his progeny. Mrs. Sadie carried a nice young hen and a dozen of her fresh eggs as a post-Easter offering to the Simmons family.

When the news of Jake's debut appeared in the Randle *Spotlight,* the town became aroused once more. Neighbors who went to Mr. Hunt's store said that Mrs. Katie said that the little Watkins boy must be one of those geniuses. She told every customer about Little Jake, showing them the article and the picture.

"He ought to travel," she concluded. "Maybe he ought to connect with one of the boy preachers. It'll be a blessing to everybody in this town."

Many of the mothers began boxing the ears of their three-year-olds and mauling their heads for not having brought fame to the Mission. Often one would say:

"There that little Jacob Benjamin Watkins singing 'Jesus Want Me for a Sunbeam' for the Lord, and you still here pulling on ninny jug."

Mrs. Sadie was regarded with new awe after the article about Little Jake appeared in the Randle *Spotlight*. It even aroused Big Jake to the point of accepting his wife's long-standing invitation to attend the Mission, though he made it no further than the back row. No one would take the chance of even reporting the mischievous deeds which Jake accumulated at the Mission, such as sticking the children with pins or sticking gum on the back of some little girl's neck — sometimes catching the fine hairs and causing pain when the teacher tried to remove it.

The only incident to disturb Mrs. Sadie's peace, a considerable time after Jake's debut, was a backyard fight which he had with Benny Thompson.

"Mrs. Sadie, he did so take my top," Benny Thompson insisted.

Mrs. Sadie pulled Benny from the ground where he straddled Jake.

"Look, honey," she told Benny, "Jake has more playthings than all of you put together at your house."

"But Mrs. Sadie, he took and hid it when we were playing blindman's bluff. I had it down there when we were spinning acorns."

"Jake, come here." Mrs. Sadie searched his pockets. After she failed to find it, she then asked him if he had taken it.

"No, ma'am," Jake crossed his heart.

Benny reached out to strike Jake again, but Mrs. Sadie stopped him.

"Now, boy, you'd better run on home," she chided Benny. "You see, Jake's got no top on him. I know he wouldn't cross his heart on a lie to me."

"He did so, Mrs. Sadie —"

"You run along, Benny."

Jake played around the yard alone until his mother was quite unaware of his actions. He felt near the root of the ivy vine, got the red top, put it together, put it in his pocket and skipped cheerfully to the privy at the end of the garden.

Jake's first school day was one for Mrs. Sadie Watkins to remember. She rose at five in the morning to prepare for the great day. She had already bought Jakes' book-bag with a lunch pocket on the side. Since she had to accompany him the first day, she decided to fix an extra lunch so that they could have enough to share with his teacher if she would accept it. She felt that her fried chicken sandwiches and chocolate cake and the pears from her own tree ought to tempt anyone's appetite.

When they reached Randle Elementary School, she felt triumphant. At last her boy would make his first decisive step toward some special goal that would make him a great man. She had already decided to take in extra washings to help buy extra needs for Little Jake and an occasional gift for his teacher.

During the assembly period Jake crouched closely to his mother. She expected that of her six-year-old boy, who had seldom been out of her sight. She was certain that he would eventually get used to being with the other children. When the assembly period ended, they went to the first grade room to register.

"This is Jacob Benjamin Watkins, Miss —"

"Miss Taylor. Now tell me your name." She smiled at Jake.

"All right, sugar, tell the teacher your name." Mrs. Sadie pulled him a little closer to Miss Taylor.

Miss Taylor touched him lightly on the shoulder to reassure him, but he moved away from her with a scowl on his face.

"Take your old black hand off me." He fought the air, not having the courage to touch the teacher.

Miss Taylor smiled halfheartedly as she spoke to Mrs. Sadie. "You know they're excited on the first day."

Mrs. Sadie felt that Jake had somehow struck his teacher the wrong way. She tried to coax him to sit at a desk in the classroom, but he followed her to the front of the room and tried to sit on the edge of her chair. Miss Taylor talked quietly to him as she escorted him to his desk once more.

In a few minutes Jake started toward his mother again. When he noticed that she had put the lunch bag on the windowsill, he spoke out.

"Mama, I'm hungry,"

"Sh-sh." The teacher put her index finger to her bottom lip and shook her head.

Jake skipped on across the floor and tried to sit on his mother's lap. When Mrs. Sadie carried him back to his seat, he started to cry. Another first-grader, who seemed older than the others, threw a spit ball, hitting Jake on the side of his head.

"Mama's baby," the boy meowed, and made ugly faces at Jake.

Miss Taylor finally whispered to Mrs. Sadie that if she left the room, Jake would perhaps learn to mingle with the other children.

Mrs. Sadie could see that the teacher lacked understanding. She spoke out to put an end to the matter.

"Miss Taylor, I see that that little boy yonder has a pick at Jake, so I might as well carry him on home with me now and let him get straight tomorrow. Then he says he's hungry."

Miss Taylor, feeling the weight of so many first-day problems gave way to Mrs. Sadie's order without objection. She expressed her joy on having met her and a desire to see her again at the P.T.A. meetings.

It was almost noon when Mrs. Sadie and Jake reached home. The distance, comparable to about eight blocks, had made her very tired. She went straight to her bedroom. Once she got inside her room, she took off her corset and stretched out on the bed with her clothes on.

"Mama," Jake tugged at her body, "I'm hungry."

"Boy, if you don't get out of here, I'll tear your hide off."

The reprimand seized Jake like the arms of an octopus — squeezing all of the warmth from his body. He sat still in his chair, striving to control the knocking within him. To him, school had not only caused him to get hit on the head with a spit ball, but had also forced him into the command of a strange dark lady. And above all, it had made his mother a mean lady. He was hungry now, and she would not give him food. He knew that if he went to the kitchen with his good clothes on, he would get a whipping.

"You sit right in that chair until I tell you to move. If you whimper, dog will be better than you." Mrs. Sadie turned her face away from him.

Little Jake knew that school had changed his wonderful world and his wonderful mother. He could not understand the sudden change.

After resting for a spell, Mrs. Sadie got up with the determination to do her duty. She undressed Jake first, then herself. She called her son, stood him up in front of her, and gave him the law.

"Jake, look here now. Don't you know that you ought not to call people black? Black is as black does. All colored people are black."

"Mama, I ain't black, and Grandma said I was her gingerbread boy. She did so."

"Don't you sass me, Jake. Maybe so, but colored people are black if they're bleached or if they're burnt, and no mind just because you didn't get so burnt that you're to call folks black. You hear me?"

"I guess so. I'm going to feed you, but mind my word," she shook her index finger at him, "if you don't do good in school, you won't be no doctor or preacher or lawyer or no kind of great man to make your mama proud of you."

"Yes, ma'am."

"Now let's eat this lunch we carried to school."

Jake nibbled halfheartedly on the food, being almost too hungry to enjoy it. He tried to play as he always did in the afternoon, but he kept thinking about the boy who hit him with the spit ball and the strange dark lady who didn't want him to talk to his mother.

The next morning Mrs. Sadie talked to Big Jake about the ordeal of the first day.

"What you want me to do?" he asked.

"What I want you to do? You ought to know your duty just like I do." Mrs. Sadie was forced to raise her voice.

"Now look, old lady, don't rile me up 'cause you and that boy been hittin' it so far while I been on the railroad." He held his wife's eyes. "Answer me, woman."

"But you ought to let him know you mean business, too." There was a plaintive tone in the woman's voice which surprised him.

"Have I ever given him any' law? I put the money in your hand. I don't raise no caine 'bout going to no church, but I ain't got no grudge against it. I like my tea. And what do I do when I get it? I don't cut up in the street. I come on home and go to sleep. What else do you want?"

"Don't you want Little Jake to be something?"

"Look, old lady, 'longs a man go his way and don't harm nobody unless it's hisself, I ain't got no ax to grind with him."

"Look, man, don't 'old lady' me to death. I know that I'm a good thirty-nine, but I still have some fight left. If you don't help me, God will, and I'll make something out of Little Jake yet."

"That's just why I didn't aim to throw in my two cents worth from the start. You got your mind made up like you had all the time. All of this talk is like writing in the sand."

Mrs. Sadie fixed Big Jake's lunch pail without saying another word. He was a good husband, a hard worker, an honest man. He was even goodlooking, if you liked a man in his mid-forties who still held his head up and kept his shoulders squared; if you liked a tall, husky man who, because of his weather-beaten tan and his brawny hands, told you that he was used to the wind and the weather and the smoke of the locomotive. She watched Big Jake as he puttered about the kitchen and the back porch. He seemed completely unaware of her eyes, which studied his every move. That was her Jake, her love, "a good catch for a black gal," her mother had said.

She started to call him as he stood quietly on the porch, but she didn't want to disturb the mood. He might be watching the early-morning sun or the color of the changing autumn leaves. She moved quietly beside him. His head was erect, but his eyes were cast downward.

"Oh, what I meant to tell you, old — I mean, Sadie — is that my papa didn't know 'A' from a bullfrog, but you couldn't cheat him out of a red penny."

"Jake, I put two slices of that chocolate cake in your lunch."

"Take care now."

Big Jake was off to his job.

Mrs. Sadie felt the weight of her feet as she walked down the steps and on across the street to the Thompsons'. She had always kept her distance from them because she had heard that Mr. Thompson's mother didn't care for dark-skinned people. This morning she forgot to care about the rumor. She had to know if Benny had shown the same signs of fear as her Little Jake on entering school. Now she thought too late that she could have sent Little Jake along with Benny and his cousin, instead of taking him herself.

Mrs. Thompson, Benny's grandmother, opened the door and invited Mrs. Sadie on to the kitchen, where she was cooking breakfast.

"Mrs. Thompson" — Mrs. Sadie spoke first — "I know I ought not to come bursting in here before you all are up and out, but I want to know how Benny's taking on to school."

"Mrs. Watkins, I thought the little fellow would talk us to death. He's crazy about school."

"I don't remember seeing him in Miss Taylor's room yesterday."

"He said that he saw you but he couldn't speak to you because they had to be quiet."

"That's right, too." Mrs. Sadie remembered Little Jake's antics.

"I always say, shove them away from your apron string as soon as possible."

"Yes'm, but you know, when they're so young and you're used to having them around you, and like me — I didn't have but one —"

"That's where you're wrong, child — well I'm old enough for your mother too —" Mrs. Thompson bent to open the oven as a tress of hair that was black and gray tumbled over her face.

Mrs. Sadie watched, saying nothing as Mrs. Thompson straightened up and threw her hair away from her face with a toss of the head.

"Lord knows I should've balled my hair before coming in the kitchen, but the time goes so fast in the morning."

"I'd better get back myself to get Little Jake up for breakfast."

"Well, the little fellow's not too far from school."

"No, ma'am." Mrs. Sadie paused, but finally stated her request.

"Mrs. Thompson, since Junius is coming by to get Benny, I wonder if Jake can go along with them to school."

"Sure, dear. Sure, you know how it is with children — the more the merrier."

"Well, I'll be seeing you, then. I'll run on and get Jake ready."

After Mrs. Sadie left Mrs. Thompson's presence, she took a deep breath. She could not love the woman, but she could not hate her. The older woman made her feel a sense of lack within herself, but she could not pinpoint the lack within herself, or the reason. She had always felt that same lack within herself on attending the Women's State Convention. Were these women different from herself? She could not always understand what they were about, but she grasped what she could in order to impress the indolent sisters of the Mission.

But one thing she knew at this point: All of Randle Town — school, church, everything — was shoddy in places. And she herself, her marriage, her ambitions — everything in her life was falling just short of the mark. The feeling of disappointment with Big Jake, nor the feeling of disappointment with Mrs. Thompson, stymied the utmost desire of her heart — the making of Little Jake.

For Little Jake, school itself had no charm except in the enjoyment of his lunches, the walk to school with Benny and his cousin, and the playground activities. All through elementary school he enjoyed himself, repeating classes occasionally but going on because his mother would have it no other way.

By the time Little Jake completed the seventh grade, Mrs. Sadie's head was half white. But she never stopped sighing and she never stopped using every ounce of her energy to get Jake cleared of his small crimes so that he could be free to go on to make himself somebody. When he was in the sixth grade, he had almost been expelled permanently for slitting two basketballs a few hours before a game, but she had paid for the balls and paid a round-trip cab-fare for the coach to make a trip to Randle High School to borrow two balls for the game. For the first time in her life Mrs. Sadie scorched one of Mr. Monegan's white shirts. It tickled Little Jake to see her all disheveled. He stood watching her as she mumbled and rubbed the scorched collar in the basin pan.

"Mama, you get all upset over every little thing. I didn't plan to cut the balls. I couldn't take a dare off Flookie."

"Who's Flookie?"

"That's that old boy what hit me with that spit ball."

"Jake, can't you all tussle and get that over with, instead of making me pay all that money?

"Maybe you couldn't, because you're aiming to be a trifling scoundrel no matter what I do. You should've been named Aaron, like your daddy's brother who's not worth his salt."

"Well, Mama, let me go to the golf course and pick up those balls and make some money."

"You go 'long, boy, before I tan your hide."

Little Jake knew that he was forgiven. He even pretended to study his lessons more seriously to reward his mother for understanding that he had no desire to work or go to school.

It was wonderful how they had learned to understand each other.

When Little Jake finally reached high school, Mrs. Sadie was sure that the change would in some way help him. Then too, Benny Thompson could help Jake with his lessons. Both of the boys were fifteen years old, but they were vastly different. Benny had a knack for getting into trouble, but Little Jake called it "story-book stuff." If the teacher sent the class to the library, Benny would lag behind to get an extra book. If they went on hikes, Benny would become interested in some sight unrelated to the hike and get lost, invariably.

Little Jake began cultivating what he called "he-man" tricks on going to high school. Truancy interested him during the first year. After being reported to the truant officer, Little Jake found school unbearable again. When, however, he found out that he would be free to leave school at the age of sixteen, he endured school until he reached the ninth grade.

Since Jake hadn't spoken to his mother concerning his knowledge of the compulsory school law, she had come to believe that he himself had found an authentic aim for attending school.

A new fear entered her mind when Benny Thompson brought a message from the principal asking that she report to his office to discuss an important matter concerning Little Jake.

"Mrs. Watkins," Professor Jenkins greeted her politely, "I've heard of your good works in the community, so I know that you don't condone your son's actions."

"What is it now, Professor Jenkins?"

"Jacob can never return to Randle High as a student, Mrs. Watkins. The School Board is behind me a hundred per cent."

"You haven't told me."

"Oh, yes." Professor Jenkins thumbed through a note pad. "He's listed with the group of youngsters who smuggled some whiskey on the campus. The janitor found them drinking it in Miss Porter's cloakroom."

"Are you sure that the janitor knows my boy, Professor Jenkins?"

"Mrs. Watkins, he didn't disturb them. He tipped me off, and I went in and took their names. I'm sorry, Mrs. Watkins."

Mrs. Sadie left Randle High School with a heavy heart. There was only one thought left to give her comfort: "Earth has no sorrow that heaven cannot heal." She decided not to scold Jake; she would pray for him to change.

The next morning she told Big Jake about the conference. He dropped his head and then cast his eyes on the floor. When Little Jake came to breakfast, she said without emotion: "You can go on and pick up those golf balls."

Little Jake looked at her, then at his father. He fixed his eyes on the scrambled eggs and shoveled them into his mouth.

Now that Little Jake had no reason to deceive his mother about school, he followed other young hoodlums about the town. Mrs. Sadie asked daily if he had found a job, so daily he spun a yarn about how he had walked and waited with no results.

Gradually rumors drifted to her that her son was frequenting Hunter's Alley. She had heard about Seymore's Joint and the terrible waste of youth in the vice niches, in murder and disease. She knew that harlots strutted freely, and gamblers threw dice and cut their dirty cards as they willed in Hunter's Alley. But Seymore's Joint was the capitol.

The idea came to her soon after the first rumor of Jake's visit to Hunter's Alley: "Call the law and have them close the Joint." She felt the need to do something. This was the solution; a way to save Jake, the answer to her prayer.

The first Sunday was Communion Day at the Mission. Usually Mrs. Sadie sang as she prepared breakfast on Sunday morning, but the Devil had crossed her terribly. Little Jake had spent his first night away from home. She fixed the good, thick brown gravy over the fried chicken, took a pan of biscuits from the stove and spanked them to see if they were spongy, and set the bubbling pot of coffee to the side.

"Big Jake," she called to her husband, "breakfast is on the stove. I've got to step off a piece."

She took her apron off, threw her gray sweater around her shoulders, and went out of the back gate. Mr. Davis' grocery store, about five blocks from her house, was the nearest place to make a telephone call. She had to rush in order to make it there and back in time to dress for the Communion services.

The morning breeze felt good against her face. The cool spell which preceded Easter always reminded her of the calm which followed all the calamities of her life — a tender quietness — a pale sadness.

Mr. Davis was busy with a customer when she arrived, but he asked to be excused and moved on to the end of the counter where Mrs. Sadie stood.

"How you, Sadie?"

"Well, I'm as well as you might expect, Mr. Davis."

"Did you want to see me on anything particular?"

"Well — yes, sir. I wonder if you'd let me use your telephone?"

"Yes — right here in town?"

"Yes, sir."

"That's a dime. You just go on there in the office and close the door. I'd 'preciate it if you didn't take too long, 'cause it's a business phone."

"Thank you, Mr. Davis."

Mrs. Sadie asked the operator to get the Chief of Police.

"Yes?" the voice on the other end asked.

"I'd like to tell you that a lot of terrible things have been going on in Hunter's Alley at that Seymore's Joint."

"Like what?" the voice asked. "Who are you?"

"I am a Christian woman who thinks the law ought to do something about closing that low-down dirty place. It's spoiling so many girls and boys."

"What're they doing, lady?" The voice seemed impatient.

"I wish you'd go see for yourself."

There was a bang on the other end. She didn't know if her call would help. Anyway she had unburdened her conscience before God and man and could partake of the Lord's Supper in peace.

Later, as they finished the communion services she sang and cried with relief as she shook a partner's hand:

> When we are sundered part
> It gives us inward pain.
> But we shall still be joined in heart,
> And hope to meet again.

"Mrs. Sadie — Mrs. Sadie." The head usher was pushing through the crowd. "The law is out here to see you."

"See me?" She moved on toward the door as the eyes of the crowd followed her.

As she put her right foot on the top step, coming down, one of the officers stepped up to meet her.

"You're Sadie Watkins?"

"Yes, sir."

"Well, I've got your boy Jake out here. We went by the house and no one was there. He said you ought to be here. Why wasn't he here with you, Aunty?"

"What's that boy gotten into now?"

"Oh, we raided Seymore's Gambling Joint, and — " Mrs. Sadie's body came toward the officer as if someone had picked her up and pitched her forward.

"Put her in our car," the officer said. "I can get her to the hospital a little faster." Mrs. Thompson went along, cradling Mrs. Sadie's head in her lap.

When Mrs. Sadie finally became aware of the fact that she was in bed, she felt too exhausted to speak. There, each sitting in a chair not far away from her bed, were Big Jake and Little Jake. As she looked at them, she almost wished that she had slept on. She was so tired. She felt as if the world had long since ended but an unkind Providence had forced her to go on after its cessation.

Big Jake pulled his chair closer to the bed to speak his words of comfort, now that his wife was awake.

"Sadie, you had one of those heart attacks, but it's none o' those bad ones. You still good as gold. The doctor told me not to tell you, but I know you like to know."

She just lay there. Both of her men seemed such perfect strangers.

Big Jake went on. "They say $100 or sixty days on the road. I went on and got the boy out. I felt you'd want him out."

She searched his eyes a full moment, then turned her face to the wall.

Runetta

"Lizzie — you, Lizzie! Come hyeah!"

"Where you, Uncle Tom?"

"Round the side."

"Sh, sh — "

"What's it, Uncle Tom?"

"Looka yonder, you ever seen anything that cute?"

"Oh, my baby."

"She's a little angel, that's what she is, I tell you."

Lizzie stood and watched Runetta as she bobbed her head, nibbling at the petals of a huge pink rose within her reach.

"Bless her little heart; she think, 'cause it's pretty, it's good to eat. No, Liz, don't you bother her, that flower ain't goin'ta hurt her. Look like nothing ought not to bother Baby Dumpling."

"I hope to goodness not, Uncle Tom. But girls are hard to raise when they don't have no daddy."

"Gal, you got this baby now, so take care of her. She's on her own two feets, and now she's in her two years, she can be left."

"I was just thinking about Grandma."

"What about your grandma?"

"Well, I'll stay on here if she don't want me."

"She ain't come for you, did she?"

"No, sir."

"And you been from the country since you was first caught up, didn't you?"

"Yes, sir."

"You know what they say? Root little pig, or die. You done good hyeah 'cause ain't no woman had her foot in hyeah since they took Anna out that front door seven years ago. A man need somebody who can make a decent pan o' biscuit bread."

"I don't know nobody much here in Randle Town, Uncle Tom."

"Like I say, soon's Baby Dumpling get good two, she can trot behind you. You git yourself to the white folks' house, where you can make yourself a living."

"Yes, sir."

"And let me tell you, you keep your dress down to them white mens, and the black ones too. You hyeah me? 'Cause what go up is bound to come down."

"Yes, sir."

"I don't want no whore under my roof."

"No, sir."

"Just like it been — If I eats, you eats, and little Puddin' too. And you do right. When I shet these eyes hyeah, I'll have it fix so no scalawag can throw you outa hyeah."

"Yes, sir."

Lizzie went around to the side of the house and watched Runetta move on to a bed of violets in the front yard. She sat in the bed, pulled a blossom, and nibbled it, but undoubtedly did not like the taste. She pulled more blooms, then flowers from the roots. Her mother picked her up quietly, kissed her, then spanked her on the hand for spoiling the bed of violets.

"You're just like Buster, that's what you are. You just mess up and tear up because you're so pretty you think everybody's going to love you anyway."

Lizzie's heart hurt as Runetta whimpered. She wanted to kiss the hand that she had spanked. She was now sixteen years old, with a baby and no husband, so she knew it was her sacred duty to chastise her little girl so that when she grew up she wouldn't make a mistake.

Her grandmother, who reared her, had started talking about a nine months' burden being a lifetime journey, but to her, that had nothing to do with the sweet little tingling sensations which she felt when Buster tumbled her on a sheet of cotton or when they wallowed in the tall rank weeds.

After cotton picking time her grandmother had called her into judgment with "Gal, is you caught up?"

She knew nothing except that morning after morning she could not keep her breakfast, and that she felt so strangely ill that she thought that she might die.

Her grandmother was no fool; besides, she had her respectability to uphold in Wedgefield. She didn't want to do anything drastic, anything wrong — or take care of a bastard grandchild.

She began a steady song around the countryside.

"Lord knows my brother Tom is in every bit of three rooms there in Debose Crossing, without a soul to hand a drink o' water. Well, if it wasn't for Lizzie, I'd be by myself, but I ain't all broke down like my brother Tom."

Soon she changed the tune:

"Lizzie's got to go yonder to Randle Town and help out that ailing brother o' mine. He ain't had a decent meal since his Anna been gone. You know that war left 'em wrong anyway."

So Lizzie was brought to her Uncle Tom Canty. Everyone consented that it was so noble for her to feel the need to care for her decrepit relative. She knew him only by name and from having seen him in the family pew at funerals.

No matter how she felt, she cooked his meals, cleaned the house, did the washing, and kept the yards swept clean.

Her grandmother had promised to get a midwife to see her through when her time came, if she cut off all connections with Buster Pringle. She declared that if she heard of his hanging around town, she would get somebody to blow his brains out if she lost her nerves. And to Lizzie, Carrie Fountain's word was law.

Lizzie's friends in the country felt that she had slipped off to marry a "no-good town boy." On hearing about her pregnancy, they decided that he had taken her cherry and abandoned her.

The neighbors in town felt that she had really done a good job of helping her uncle, but took her husband to be a brute who let his young wife slave for an uncle.

When they could find no young man coming or going, no matter what time they peeped under the shades, they figured that some man had just "left his load."

Lizzie was able to get a job at Mrs. Otto's house when Runetta was three years old.

She had thought of several ways of bringing a man into her life, but no way seemed the right way. Her little girl called her great-grand-uncle "Papa," as she heard other men called in their homes. This, she decided, would have to do until the course of Runetta's life forced her to make some type of adjustment.

She joined the Mission and carried Runetta to Sunday School and church every other Sunday.

Runetta was unanimously voted to be the prettiest child who attended the Mission. When she started attending Randle Elementary School, the same chorus of "pretty girl," "pretty girl," gave Runetta the idea that she must be special in some way. Therefore, she made friends with the little girls who wore the prettiest clothes and brought the best lunches. When the first grade gave its closing exercise, she, along with her friends, were raindrops.

She wore a white, sleeveless dress made of crepe paper, with huge golden circles imprinted on the skirt. A chorus sang "See the Little Raindrops" as they dipped and twirled into designs which the teacher had traced lightly on the floor.

After the program, the children went to the closest classroom to change their clothes. The mothers went in to help, while the fathers stood in the hall waiting to help with the packages.

Runetta stared hungrily at the little girls who ran to their fathers. Janie Sue's father lifted her from the floor and carried her all the way down the stairs.

"Your daddy didn't want you to be no raindrop, Netta?" Janie Sue asked the next day.

Runetta did not know what to say.

"He didn't come to see you?"

"My mama came."

"My mama came, and my sister and my brother and my aunt and my granny what brought me."

"My papa'll come," Runetta said.

Eventually she came home with news from the outside that she did not have a daddy.

"How come, Mama, I'm a Taylor and you a Taylor and Papa a Canty and Big Mama a Fountain?"

Lizzie had one answer for all such queries: "I see you want a stepdaddy."

"No'm, I don't want no stepdaddy."

Each time Runetta asked a question concerning her father, Lizzie renewed her determination to make herself an example for Runetta. Maybe then Runetta would not grow up to be spoiled by any young fellow.

As Runetta grew up, Lizzie's uncle became worried because she never tried to get a husband.

"Gal," he reminded her, "you work hard and you take care of Puddin', but you need a man. Take me, now; I can't do no cuttin' up, but if I could, you'd hyeah from me."

But Lizzie Taylor kept her resolve with the hope that her ordered life would encourage Runetta to be a good girl. One day she could have a wedding for her, as Mrs. Otto had had for her daughter. There would be flowers everywhere and enough ice cream and cake for all of the neighbors. And there would be a son-in-law and many babies to cuddle. If she did not get a husband for herself, she could fill her life with Runetta's living.

Runetta was one of three youngsters from the Mission to attend Randle High School. She had begun to get tired of the fellows who looked at her as she might have been something good to eat before she left Randle Elementary School. She had not been interested in such common flirtations. She looked forward to meeting a fellow that she could brag about. She wanted to meet a boy who would have real manners, like her mother's employer. Mr. Otto ran the best jewelry store on Main Street in Randle Town, so he never put on overalls or rough work pants. He never wore big, rusty, clumping, muddy shoes.

Mrs. Otto worked at the Citizens Bank, so no one stayed at the house during the day after her daughter had married and left town. Lizzie was left in charge, so Runetta had the chance to explore the house carefully — room by room, closets, shelves, drawers.

She liked the delicate scents which gushed to her nostrils as she pulled open a drawer full of underthings. Her mother isolated these pieces from the other laundry and sponged them with tender care. It was her duty to press them with a warm iron after they had dried.

Runetta liked most of the food that was served at the house. The heavily buttered toast was always a little tuggy when she strove to bite it, but she liked the sensation of the struggle.

Sometimes they carried a pan of food to their home to share with the neighbors. Many ate the food halfheartedly, proclaiming, "This ain't nothing but mess." Such an occasion gave Runetta the chance to display her superior taste.

Often she would say, "Mrs. Otto fixed the best old spinach," when she could not stand the sight or the taste of it. Again she would say, "Mrs. Otto fixed the best old egg custard," when she gagged even as she washed the mixing bowl.

The summer of 1938 made Mrs. Otto's house the most interesting place in the world. Her niece from Jacksonville, Florida, spent her entire summer vacation in Randle Town.

Runetta helped Margaret to unpack her bags, and for the first time it struck her that she might never have all of the pretty things that she desired. The people at the Mission got rigged up in their Sunday clothes, but they looked so ugly to her all of the rest of the week. Life in her sphere was so ugly. Everything about her home community was so different from the home that she and her mother worked in on Broad Street.

On the slightest provocation, Margaret would give Runetta dresses, blouses, slips, beads, shoes — anything, in fact, since she didn't particularly want to force her aunt to buy new clothes to replace the old things. It usually worked.

Each gift pleased Runetta, for she visualized the hateful, yet admiring, stares which would follow her as she walked into the Mission on Sunday morning. She would often ask her mother why the tips of the preacher's collar turned up on the end and why his shoes were dusty every Sunday morning.

"All right now, baby, don't you go talking about the man who carry the gospel, just because you not saved. Watch your mouth."

"I guess he's all right, Mama," she replied.

"That's not the way Windell says their preacher look."

"Who's Windell, Baby?"

Lizzie knew that Runetta talked to the fellows, but it made her feel uneasy to hear her single out one in particular.

A new shadow crossed her view.

She knew at that moment that she should tell her daughter about life, but she didn't know how to start. Maybe Runetta would want to know how a woman had a baby. No matter what happened, she knew that she could never sit across the table and say, "Baby, now that you're seeing yourself, you better not have no boys fumbling under your skirt." Maybe at school the teachers had a different way of telling the young people about everything, so she would leave it up to them.

"You sick, Mama?"

"Oh no, Baby. Where's Windell's house?"

"Across the track on Lloyd Street."

"How you know him?"

"He's in my class. We sit on the second seat of the first row because we have 92."

"I'm so glad you studying, Baby."

"Mama, I want to wear my wide-tailed pea-green taffety dress Margaret gave me to church Sunday, but you have to help me hem it up."

"What's today?"

"It's Thursday, so you don't have to rush."

"I know I'm paying you for making 92, but that's all right, so long as you don't let boys go to your head."

"Mama!"

On Sunday, Runetta wore her pea-green taffeta dress, which made a rustling sound as she swirled down the aisle of the Mission. She had made it her business to come in after the pastor's prayer, knowing that most of the backless plank benches would be filled. She went closer than usual to the front, all eyes following her.

When Reverend Gates called for joiners, she walked straight to the front and gave him her hand. As soon as she relinquished her feeling of triumph on seeing the eyes feast on her dress, a queer sensation ran up and down her spine as she listened to the words of the song the audience sang:

> Where shall I be
> When the first trumpet sound?
> Where shall I be
> When it sound so loud
> It sound so loud
> Till it wake up the dead.
> Where shall I be when it sound?
> I want to be in Glory
> When the first trumpet sound
> I want to be in Glory
> When it sound so loud,
> It sound so loud,
> Till it wake up the dead.
> Where shall I be when it sound?

The congregation paused to hear her testimony.

Runetta stood, her small lips quivering and her hazy-brown eyes glassy with tears that she would not let fall.

Deacon Cummings began his usual questioning:

"You know Christ 'n pardon your sins?"

She bobbed her head.

"What you seen, child?"

Runetta pulled the sash around her dress with her right hand and combed her soft brown hair with the other hand.

Deacon Cummings became distracted as he watched the girl's hair fall carelessly back in place as she moved her fingers up and down.

"You hear anything, child?"

She fastened her eyes to the floor. Deacon Cummings' eyes glanced downward. He noticed the slender ankles rocking in the patent-leather slippers. Her snow-white anklets hugged the olive-brown skin which seemed too delicate to touch.

"Lord . . ." He took a hard swallow.

Facing the audience again, he called for a motion to accept Sister Runetta Taylor as a candidate for baptism. She seemed to be too full of the spirit to utter a word. He had examined such converts before.

He got a second for his motion.

On her way from Mrs. Otto's house, Lizzie Taylor heard that Runetta had joined the church. She felt no sense of the exhilaration that she had thought she would feel when her daughter joined the church. She had been cheated out of the moment which the Mission mothers relished next to the marriage ceremony. Somehow she could not help but feel the slight, for Runetta was fifteen years old and should have had the kindness to select a Sunday when her mother was off from work.

Finally she made herself believe that the spirit might have forced the child to surrender herself; therefore, she herself might have been at fault in hoping that this mystery might work to her advantage. She would look forward to the baptismal service, which she could plan on with surety.

Lizzie never questioned Runetta closely about her personal affairs as her grandmother had done. She had to accept Runetta's refusal to be baptized.

"Mama, I've come sick, so I can't get in all that water, can I?" she asked.

"Oh, no, Baby," she hastened to answer.

She almost believed with the neighbors that Runetta had joined the church to show the pea-green taffeta dress which Margaret had given her.

But Windell had really caused Runetta to change her mind. He told her how the minister of Wesley Methodist Church sprinkled water over each candidate's head — not even enough to make the person wet. They didn't have to go in a whole pool of water. She felt that she would rather be in that type of church, though she had never attended one.

"Windell," she asked, "if I go under that water and then want to join a church like yours, will they let me in?"

"They might," he said. "You just ought not to get all wet in that pool."

So she told her mother about her "sickness," knowing that she would be excused from the ceremony.

When the neighbors started going to the church for the baptismal services, Lizzie gave up her corner in the swing and went into the bedroom to lie down. This was unusual.

Runetta sat a little longer, pumping the swing to sail farther into the air. Sally Jones, one of the candidates, paused at the gate to ask if she were ready.

"Not yet," she told Sally.

Deep within her heart she wanted to please her mother, but everything was so ugly around them. She could not understand the Lord. She had often asked her mother why they couldn't have some of the pretty things that Mrs. Otto had. Mrs. Otto did not even attend church.

If they did not have all the things that the people on Broad Street could afford, she wanted to know why they could not live across the track, where Windell lived. The streets were paved; there were lights on every corner that stayed on all night. The trash man came by, and the mailman put letters in a box on the porch.

Windell talked about the Society meetings which his mother attended, and the Silver Teas which she gave. She was the secretary of the Willing Workers Club, which donated food and clothes to needy families during the Christmas season. Sometimes he brought goodies to her on Monday that he had saved from Sunday. Had she not gone to Mrs. Otto's house with her mother, she would not have been able to recognize Windell's gifts.

She made a pledge to herself that she would be as sweet and clean as she could be, and that she would work hard to make herself pretty so that Windell would like her even though her people were different from his in some respects.

But, deep within her heart, she wanted to please her mother. She had told Sally that she would come later; and this she would do. She went into the bedroom and tickled her mother's toes.

"Stop, Baby." Lizzie was really not provoked.

"Mama, you call me 'Baby.' They call me 'Netta' at school."

"You're my baby."

"All right, then. Mama, your baby wants to go to church."

"You know —"

"We can see the other children."

"You little devil. You not shame?"

"No'm."

"Maybe we'll get there time enough to get a seat."

The sun went down, leaving a scarlet line close to the edge of the land far behind the Mission. As they walked in the door, the first candidate was being led to the pool, which was beneath the little choir stand.

The congregation had started the hymn "Let's Go Down to Jordan and Be Saved."

As the eyes turned back to meet them, she pinched her mother's arm. Lizzie looked down and smiled.

As winter approached, Lizzie bought Runetta's new underclothes for the season. She bought four pairs of knee-length bloomers, four undershirts with elbow-length sleeves, two gray knitted-wool slips, and two white cotton slips.

Instead of hugging her mother when she opened the package, Runetta backed away. The tears met under her chin.

"Baby, what's the matter?"

"Mama, Gertie and Willie Mae don't wear those old long bloomers and undershirts. They say you'll smell bad."

"Baby, you can wash good and rub a little baking soda under your arm."

"Mama, I have something called 'Mum,' but you still don't smell good."

"Now, you listen to me. I'm not having you catch your death o' cold just because those little man-hungry gals want you to go half-naked in the winter. Come the fifteenth of October, you put on a knitted slip, your undershirt and some knee socks and those bloomers."

Runetta had never known her mother to be so rash. She wondered if Windell's mother wore such ugly underthings. She guessed that her teacher didn't wear such oldfashioned things. Undoubtedly she wore jersey bloomers like Mrs. Otto, because she looked trim all the winter. Reverend Gates' wife seemed to gain twenty-five pounds after the first frost. The favorite conversations of the women hinged on this topic.

"It's scandalous," Mrs. Vicey used to say.

"What I got under here. I won't freeze — anything, I might suffocate."

Being on the outskirts of the whole wide world was more than often the cause of a restless night. "Why? Why? Why? Why? was all that an annoying voice whispered in Runetta's ear as she twisted and tumbled in her bed.

The food also changed in her home when winter came. She wanted a bowl of corn flakes for breakfast, or buttered toast and jelly with a glass of milk.

"Baby, what's come upon you all of a sudden? Now, it's bad enough to eat such mess in warm weather; but now's cold, you need something substantial between your ribs. You face the north wind going to school."

Runetta began her revolt without a word of dissent. She refused to eat the grits and gravy and puffy biscuits. She would nibble on her bit of sausage or bacon, then slip away.

Her revolt against the woolen slips and the undershirts was planned with equal quiet.

Runetta had a speaking part in the Thanksgiving play. She would not tell her mother, because she wanted to wear her pea-green taffeta dress, which would not fit over the undershirt and the wool slip. She wore a regular school outfit, but carried her other dress along in order to change in the cloakroom during the recess hour. When she changed clothes, she rolled her slip and the undershirt up neatly, and put them into her sewing bag.

She felt so light, so free. For the first time Windell would see her in Sunday clothes.

When Windell offered to carry her books, walking her to the corner of Oriole and Pike, which severed him from his usual gang, she knew that the little green taffeta dress had done its duty.

She resolved, next, to wear her anklets to school rather than the knee socks.

On the way to school, there was a vacant lot where a house had burned, leaving tall, now wild, evergreen hedges. Runetta went ahead of the crowd so that she would have time to change socks.

The boys admired her; the girls envied her. She soon felt confident enough to brag about the tricks she played on her mother and her Uncle Tom.

She watched herself in the mirror whenever she had a spare minute, and worked out point by point the little things that she could do to make herself prettier.

Frequently her mother asked if she were wearing enough clothes, and she always assured her mother that she was nice and warm.

Runetta had a role in the Christmas play, too. She was the angel who said:

> Fear not, for behold, I bring you good tidings
> of great joy . . . for unto you is born this day
> in the City of David, a Savior, who is Christ
> the Lord.

She wanted to look like an angel. She wanted her hair to be clean and shiny and curled to fall about her shoulders with a careless gracefulness. She wanted some good vanishing cream, so that her face would be "silky smooth." She would practice her movements so that she could float on the stage, fold her hands, and smile just enough to spread a halo on her face. And Windell's mother would marvel at her beauty, even though she did not have a father or a splendid house.

She wondered what her mother would say to Windell's mother. She wondered if they would stand there examining each other's clothes until they both walked away feeling that they had been undressed.

Windell's mother, she knew, must be a high-brown with a

pretty enough face but cold eyes which might chill the person she examined. She might have a ball of hair on the back of her neck or on the top of her head. She might sit very erect because of a stiff corset. Her mother was a high-brown, too, but she had never taken time to primp. Her clothes never seemed to be quite comfortable, or the colors just right. The dark circles under her eyes bespoke weariness.

Runetta's reverie of the mothers' meeting was broken, along with the angel image of herself, when she discovered that she had "come sick" two days before the Christmas program. Her hair was dusty because she had swept the yard bareheaded. She could not be an angel without shiny hair.

Lizzie had told Runetta continually to avoid bathing her entire body, soaking her feet, or washing her hair during her sickness. But the Christmas program was a special affair. The girl decided that the Good God would have to make an exception. She had to be a beautiful angel for her mother, for Windell and *his* mother. She knew that her mother would say, "Baby, you were a pretty enough angel to be in heaven." And she would feel the longing for a father a whole minute before embracing her mother.

"Next year," she told herself. "I'll be sweet sixteen, so Windell can come to my house every Sunday night."

On the night of December twenty-second, Lizzie and Runetta crunched through a heavy blanket of snow to reach Randle High School. As they walked along, thoughts of the old wives' tale haunted her. Maybe it was true that your brains would burst if the blood rushed to your head. Maybe she should not have disobeyed her mother's rule. She should not have washed her hair the wrong time of the month.

She went through the angel role with a heavy head. Windell had pinched her on the arm just before he donned his shepherd's costume, but it did not tickle her flesh — there was a dull ache, instead.

Runetta usually asked her mother to buy refreshments after the program, since it gave her the time to talk with her classmates and to see their parents. They would congregate in little groups, eating hot dogs or hamburgers, carefully to avoid smearing their Sunday clothes. Sometimes they could have a Nehi drink or an ice cream cone also.

This privilege made her aware of the peculiar attitude taken by most of the other parents in her community. They simply ignored the refreshment stand. Sometimes an anxious youngster tugged after the mother's arm, only to receive the sentence: "You not going to stuff your stomach tight with that trash, when I got some t' eat at home." The sad eyes would watch the refreshment table while the feet followed the parent, until at last the feet passed through the door and the sad eyes had to go in the same direction as the feet.

But this night, Runetta wanted to go home. When her mother asked if she were sick, she merely told her that she had become "sick" for the month.

As they walked home across the crisp snow, Runetta quivered. She put her hands in her coat pockets and raised the collar up to her ears. Chills shook her so terribly that her teeth chattered. Wher her mother asked if she were cold, she shook her head, holding her tongue, biting it to keep her teeth from touching. She squeezed the muscles of her stomach to avoid trembling.

As they neared the house, she wanted to say, "Mama, I bathed all over and washed my hair after I came sick." Instead, she decided to keep her secret.

On reaching home, she went straight to the kitchen to smuggle the bottle of St. Joseph's oil. She mixed a tablespoon of sugar, salt and soda together, then tied it in the corner of her clean hankerchief. When, pretending sleep, she heard her mother's steady breathing, she undressed in front of the fireplace and massaged her temples, chest and sides as best she could with the oil. She dressed in her outing gown and went to bed. She sucked the mixture in the hankerchief to clear her throat.

Lizzie fell to sleep almost always as soon as she got in bed. She had intended to tell Runetta once more that she had been the cutest angel in the play, though she had stammered something about it once or twice.

After a first, sound nap, Lizzie became restless. She drifted in and out of a dream.

Runetta's hair fell about her shoulders just as it had done in the angel scene, but instead of her having a white sheet draped about her, she wore a white chiffon dress. She floated around the mirror but would come to the bed to ask, "Is it time yet, Mama?" She would drift away again, only to return with the same question. The last time, she paused before the mirror, holding a bunch of violets in her hand. She began strewing the violets about the room, smiling just as she always had done on having her way. A man that she could not identify came to the door, beckoned to Runetta, and announced:

"Yes, it's time."

"Baby!"

Lizzie woke with a start. She had to stop her child. She should not go to the stranger who was dressed in a dark suit, a white shirt and a dark tie. If Runetta were going to marry him, he should not have seen her in the wedding dress.

She sat up in bed, recognizing hèr confusion as the cold room chilled her. She had been daydreaming. No man had been in the room. Runetta was quiet in her bed. She regretted that Runetta had stopped sleeping with her. Margaret had become so exasperated, when she learned that they slept together, that she had to buy a single iron bed for each of them to please Runetta.

Any fool knew that dreaming about white, purple or black was the sign of death. She could think of no one who was ill in the family or in the neighborhood, but she knew that the implication of her dream was as sure as life itself. She decided against checking the cover on her daughter's bed.

Lizzie went on to work, the morning of the twenty-third, after leaving word with her uncle to tell Runetta to pump two tubs full of water and to fill the wash pot in the yard also.

When Runetta failed to stir by ten o'clock, Tom Canty decided to waken her. He called several times from the kitchen, but she did not answer.

"Impident little hussy. She hyeah me," he mumbled.

He seldom ventured into the women's room, but he would not allow a child that he had favored even before her birth to ignore him. He walked to the bed, pulled the cover from her face and shook her. She frowned as she tried to cough. Her face twisted in pain. He went back to his room and got his bottle of whiskey and rock candy.

"Hyeah, sit up, gal. Your mammy may not like it, but you got to break that cold. Hyeah, you sip this now."

She paid no attention to him.

He went to the kitchen to get a tablespoon. He opened her lips halfway, and tilted the liquid to her parted lips. It dribbled on the pillowcase.

"Well, now, she must be sick."

Tom Canty put on his old top coat and hat, got his stick, and did not stop to light his pipe until he reached Mrs. Otto's backdoor.

Lizzie's heart jumped in her mouth when she saw her uncle.

"Look hyeah, I don't know what to do with that gal o' yourn. You know I ain't nothing with wemmin-folks."

Lizzie rolled the excess flour from her hands and started untying her apron. She never thought about the meal she was in the process of preparing until three weeks later. One of Mrs. Otto's neighbors told her that she had found the meat in the oven burned to charcoal.

Tom Canty and Lizzie stopped by Dr. Felder's house, but he was out on a call. The neighbors brought their tallow, castor oil, turpentine and senna-leaf tea. Mrs. Vicey placed a saucer of turpentine under the center of the bed to kill the fever. Whatever Runetta said was unintelligible, so they were sure that she did have the fever.

"Double pneumonia."

"What must I do, Dr. Felder?"

"Keep the room warm and follow the instructions on the prescription when you fill it."

"Thank you, Doctor."

She had to keep an even temperature in a room with a fireplace. She had to keep it warm, so she stuffed the keyholes, the cracks in the ceiling and the gaps around the window sills with cotton to bar the outside air.

The women from the Mission helped by sitting up at night. Several men helped by cutting back logs. No one mentioned it outright, but they all looked forward to the ninth day, which would determine whether Runetta would improve. They had witnessed some measure of improvement but the ninth day was the authentic turning-point.

On the morning of December thirtieth, Lizzie arose before Mrs. Birdie Ealey gave up her night post. She knew that Runetta would be better.

Somehow she knew that her God would not give her a cross that she could not bear. She had denied herself pleasures that were supposedly due all young women to rear her child in an upright manner. She had longed to see Buster despite her grandmother's threat, but she had obeyed the orders given her, so that all of them could see that she was not a bad woman. But Buster had never made an effort to see her after she left Wedgefield. She had heard that a man would risk his life to see his family if he really cared. He had never written a letter, nor had he expressed an interest in seeing the child that he had fathered.

She went to the kitchen to make fire in the stove so that she could have warm water for Runetta's sponge bath. Soon after, she returned to the bedroom; Runetta made an effort to sit up in bed. The cover was too heavy for her to move, so Mrs. Birdie pulled it back. Runetta yawned.

The thought came to Lizzie's mind in a second: if a very sick person yawned, it was a sure sign that he would recover. She would fix a big breakfast.

"Mama?"

"Yes, Baby."

"Is Christmas gone?"

"Yes, but your Santa Claus is here."

"Why didn't you wake me up so I would know it, Mama?"

"No — when a sick person is sleeping, it's a help to them getting well, so it's best not to wake them."

"Can Mrs. Birdie help me up in a little while?"

"Yes, Baby."

Mrs. Birdie gave Runetta a sponge bath before the fireplace and dressed her in a clean blue outing gown. She combed her hair, sprinkled talcum powder in her bosom and down her back, and then brought the Christmas presents.

Runetta examined the new baby-pink silk underskirt. It was the first one that she had ever had.

"That's Mrs. Otto's Christmas."

"It feels good." She caressed it with her cheek.

"I told him to bring you these three and a half yards of blue taffety, this red tam and these red anklets."

Runetta sat in the big rocking chair wrapped up in a blanket, hugging her gifts.

"Is school started, Mama?"

"No, you must be thinking about that Windell."

School seemed so far in the past. She remembered that Windell had promised to slip a present to her after the Christmas program, but they had rushed away because her head was splitting. She asked to go back to bed after eating a baked apple.

She could smell sickness in her bed. It was all about her person. She wished to be in her silk slip, blue taffeta dress and red tam in the aisle of the Mission, moving toward the front seat. She drifted into sleep, feeling the eyes of the members upon her new outfit.

At five o'clock that afternoon, Lizzie roused her patient to sit her on the chamber pot, to wipe her hands and face, and to give her a bowl of broth.

"You want anything else before I give you your medicine?"

"No'm."

"Say your prayers."

"Yes'm."

Word got around that Runetta had changed for the better, so none of the women came to sit through the night.

Lizzie was awakened the next morning by an insistent knock on the door.

"Lizzie, Lizzie."

It was her Uncle Tom.

"I got a bag o' ernges for the gal."

The clock on the mantlepiece said 9:47. She never allowed herself to sleep later than seven. The air in the room nipped her nose. The big oak back-log had burned to ashes.

"Uncle Tom."

"What say?"

"Please, sir, start me a blaze in the fireplace, since you're up."

"Just made a fire in the stove. Cain't do without Uncle Tom, eh?"

"I'm used to the fire all night. I don't want to get sick, too."

"Hush up, gal, I know wemmin."

After the room became warm, Lizzie decided to waken Runetta.

"Baby, Baby." She began pulling the cover away, the five quilts and the two blankets.

"Baby!"

There her child lay, a waxen mold.

The Shadow Between Them

Michael was five years old when he asked his mother if people could bite with their eyes. She thought that it was such a bright idea — such an imponderable question — that she never got tired of repeating it. She would also laugh five full minutes whenever she reported the instance, whether anyone else seemed impressed or not.

Three years passed before she asked if anyone had "bitten" him with their eyes. He told her no, even though he had become more and more conscious of a response within himself to a hostile glance. But he had not been overly concerned with himself to begin with. He had seen a look in Josie's eyes, when she stared at his mother, which he had tried to interpret even at the age of five.

After sticking his thigh accidentally with a penknife Josie gave him for his eleventh birthday, he could identify the response to the glance as a sharp, quick stab in the heart. He kept this knowledge to himself even when Josie, Sweet Josie, threw the glance at him. She was considered to be his second grandmother, his mother's greatest friend and a blessing to Wedgefield. His mother said that Josie had started helping her father run his neighborhood grocery store when she was a girl of ten, and had helped until he died. She was known to slip candy and cookies to the children who could not buy sweets, and other items in the store to the people who were considered needy in the neighborhood.

By the time she inherited the store at the age of twenty-seven, the people said that she was set on being a spinster. She had made a vow to help the needy to help themselves. A husband, she declared, might prevent her from realizing her dream. Some said that Josie felt that no man in Wedgefield was good enough for her or her business, but no one had the nerve to repeat this version directly to her. When she walked down the street, the freckles flecking her red face, and her copper hair piled in a bun on the top of her head, the men took off their hats to her and women made pleasant-enough smiles on their lips.

When her business began to grow, she made up her mind to hire a clerk and a delivery boy. She wanted them to be needy, but she also wanted them to be deserving. She wanted the clerk to be a girl who could also set down what people took up, and figure well enough to avoid hard feelings about their accounts. She wanted a boy who was not ashamed to deliver groceries on a regular bicycle.

She heard people talking about the hard time Pay Dozier was having with her seven children; still, she heard that they had better report cards than any other children in the neighborhood. One morning Pay's children told her that a bright-skinned lady with a ball of hair on the top of her head was coming down the path. Pay knew that it was Sweet Josie.

Josie told Pay that she wanted Milly and Bo for her clerk and delivery boy.

"I'll treat the children just like my own," she promised, "and I'll trust them as long as they trust themselves."

From that day on, Milly and Bo were called Josie's children. And when Milly married and gave birth to Michael, she claimed him as her own, too.

Milly knew that Michael had no special love for Josie. Though he knew of the legend of kindness which gave his mother a start in life, he invented a different excuse to stay at home every time she encouraged him to visit Josie. Most of all he hated her three-word lecture that came the minute after she kissed him ("Don't touch anything"), whenever he was going to Josie's; and next of all, taking a lunch bag. He didn't mind the fifty-cent piece too much, though.

For no reason at all, as far as Milly could tell, Michael became ill. He complained about a pain that was in his chest. The family doctor could find nothing wrong with him, though the boy insisted that his heart was hurting. Milly had not worked away from home since her marriage because, with her husband in the Army and out of the country, she felt the urge to make up for his absence by giving all of her time to Michael. At this point, however, she could not stretch her budget to pay fees to a heart specialist, so she decided to work on Saturday as a part-time clerk to pay Michael's doctor bill. Josie volunteered to take care of the boy each Saturday.

When she told Michael that she would take him out of school to take him to a heart specialist on Friday, he slipped away to school. She explained the situation to the principal, so he allowed her to take him out of class. The initial examination indicated that nothing was wrong with Michael's heart. Milly agreed, however, for him to be submitted to the hospital for extensive testing in the event the symptoms recurred. She decided to accept her part-time job just the same, since Josie would care for Michael.

"It's time to go to Josie," she reminded him after they finished breakfast on Saturday morning. "And here's your lunch and your money. Oh — don't touch anything."

"I'm not going to stay home," he replied. "I'm almost twelve years old; I don't need that old woman to take care of me."

"She's sixty-nine, all right, but she can get around as well as people in their thirties," she argued. "I don't have to defend Josie, anyway. You take your lunch and this money and march over there as I told you." She raised her voice higher than usual. Michael flung the lunch bag across the table, and the half dollar on the floor.

"Your tongue is just like Josie's eyes!" he yelled. "You're making my heart hurt."

"Whatever are you talking about, boy? Put your hand on the spot that hurts you," she demanded.

"That's all right," he said.

"No, it's not all right," she replied. "You have rebelled against your own mother, who is willing to sacrifice her time and all to help you even though the doctor says you're not sick. Besides, you don't seem to have any respect for Josie even though she loves you like a grandmother. You listen now — I won't stand this, because she's the best friend we have in Wedgefield, or in the U.S.A., for that matter."

"I don't like her, and so I'm not going to stay over there. I want to stay home."

"Josie says you're apt to get in devilment, and you might do that if I turn my back. You know you're just eleven, not twenty-one. You could at least pretend that you like her for my sake, couldn't you?" she asked.

"No, I don't like her. And she doesn't like you. She has eaten you up with her eyes — no, bitten you up." He had forgotten his old description. "Now she's on me."

"If you aren't the craziest boy! You'll have to tell me what you mean."

"I don't really know, but she doesn't like us, so we ought not to go over there."

"We, Michael?"

"She looks at me now that way she looks at you."

"What do you mean?" She asked. "How does she look at us?"

"I'll tell you about me. And I know you'll punish me because I'm not to play baseball in the street with Pee Wee and Snukum, but I like it. We were out there playing in the street and I found a five-dollar bill in the sand — honest I did."

"Five dollars — and you didn't even give it to me, and I have such a tight budget?"

"That was a long time ago, about three months," Michael confessed.

"So you sneaked around and spent it for foolishness, when I can hardly make ends meet since your daddy forces me to save more than we're able to so that we can buy a bigger house when he's out of the Army."

"You're making my heart hurt," he told his mother, "just like Josie's eyes."

"It should hurt Michael," she said, and then she went to hug him when she realized she had said the wrong thing.

"No, I don't love Josie. And I won't love you any more, because you want my heart to hurt," replied Michael.

"What about Josie? Didn't I ask you that before?" she exclaimed.

This time he told her, not to relieve her curiosity but to hurt her because she undoubtedly wanted him to hurt inside.

"I forgot about playing in the road when I wasn't supposed to so I went running to the store and told Josie what I'd found. A lady was in the store, so Josie said, 'You're a lucky boy.' And then she looked at me the way I've seen her look at you all the time."

"Go ahead," his mother urged.

"When the lady left, she called me and said, 'I was hoping not, but I knew you'd be like them.' Them? 'Who?' I asked her. 'Milly and Bo, that's who,' she said. 'You're going to be rogues from one generation to the other. Where's that money?' she said, and stood over me with her hand in the air. 'In my pocket,' I said, and held it out. She yelled, 'Give it to me!' and I ducked her."

"Did you let her take it after all? I know you did," she answered.

"She made me give it to her. She said that I had stolen it out of her billfolder, and made out that I found it and was going to set Pee Wee and Snukum up to stand by my lie."

"Did you take it out of her billfolder, honey?"

"Me? I don't steal, Mother."

"I just asked to be sure."

"I thought you loved me and you'd know I don't steal."

"Boys do things for mischief sometimes," she said. "But if you said you didn't steal it, I guess you didn't."

"So since then," Michael concluded, "she's been looking at me the way she looks at you. I don't want to go over there anymore."

"I'll talk to her and it ought to be all right. And I want you to be there when I talk to her. I'm going on to work now. You take care and don't be bad. Just stay right here in the house and the yard and don't let anybody come here to play with you. You hear me, Michael?" she asked.

"Yes, Mother," he answered, and watched her walk away.

On Sunday, after church, they went to see Josie. She served them the best home-made pound cake and vanilla ice cream that a body could get in Wedgefield. When they had finished, Milly spoke to Josie in a level voice, inquiring about a matter which had lingered in her mind since the first day she and Bo came to work in the store.

"Josie . . ." she paused briefly. "I am a coward. I should have told you the truth years ago, but I felt guilty because you accused us. Really, we were innocent. Hungry, but innocent."

"Whatever are you talking about?" Josie asked, fastening her sharp eyes on Milly's face.

"You don't remember?"

"Remember what, sugar?" she asked with just piety.

"Just about two hours after you hired us, you went to the house. I really thought that you went because you had to. I didn't know that you went because you expected Bo and me to steal because we were hungry."

"I didn't know you-all were hungry, sugar."

"Josie, you know everybody in Wedgefield knew that we were hungry more days than we were full."

"That's what was said, but I couldn't say for sure that you were hungry the day I hired you."

"But we were. We were hungry. I could hide mine, and I

would have all day, but Bo was only ten; he just couldn't. When the bakery truck brought the order, Bo fastened his eyes on a stack of cinnamon buns. A look came into his face as if an angel right from heaven stood before him. You can blame me, but something tore at my heart string when I saw that look on his face.

" 'Bo,' " I said, " 'I'm the clerk. You can take up a cinnamon bun, a half pound of bologna and a Pepsi-Cola. You're my first customer in this new ledger.' I had cut the bologna and he had opened the Pepsi-Cola — you remember, as I picked up the cinnamon bun off the top of the counter and handed it to him and looked around, you stood on the porch shaking your finger and saying, 'I see you.' Bo was so busy eating that he never knew what passed between us. I had it on the book when you came in and you saw it, but I was sure you figured that I put it there after you accused me. I guess you figured I didn't even put down the right amounts. Now you've accused my child."

"Milly, your judgment now is just as poor as it was then. All you had to do was to tell me. Just like Michael, all he had to do was to tell me that he took the money from my purse. I probably wouldn't have told you, and you know that I wouldn't lay a hand on your child." Josie cut another slice of cake for herself.

"You have laid a hand on him, all right. And you should give him the five dollars. I'm asking you to because I know he's telling the truth. Pee Wee and Snukum helped to prove his innocence."

"You're all excited, Milly, when none of this doesn't matter. You and Bo worked for me until the business forced me to get a partner. And we've lost nothing because of the little incident." Josie put on her maternal smile.

"Maybe you haven't," Milly answered, "but what about me?"

"You brought it on yourself, sugar," she said. "But you haven't learned too much yet. Eleven-year-old boys don't go about picking up five-dollar bills in the sand."

"So you don't intend to give him his money, Josie?"

"No. He's afraid that I'll be mean if he confesses, but I won't. I'll be just as nice to him as I have been to you and Bo all of these years."

"But Michael had no right to steal. I give him a lunch and money to buy drinks and candy from the store every single time I leave him with you."

"Milly, you're the same as my child, but I see that you don't understand. So let's drop it, sugar. In fact, none of this should've been discussed before this child anyway. Do you-all want any more cake and ice cream?"

"No," Michael answered before Milly could speak, "I don't ever want any more of your cake and ice cream. I want my money, Josie, and you won't give it to me."

"Don't you worry, Michael." Milly walked toward him. Suddenly he started backing away from her. "I'll give you five dollars."

"No," he said, "I don't want it — not even from you."

The two women looked at each other. The pain deepened in Milly's eyes as Josie smiled and patted the mingled-gray ball on the top of her head.

Return of the Spouse

Tole uŝed the signal when he knocked on Penny Motts' front door. He had reached front-door status before going on the road, so he could think of no reason to do otherwise now, because he had been gone only ninety days.

After repeating the signal five times in a row, he became discouraged and started to walk away. Just before he reached the steps, Penny's voice called out.

"Who knock?"

He could not call his own name.

"Who knock, I say. If you can't speak," she said, "I got me something in here that will."

"Me," he answered.

"Me, who?" She mocked his tone. "If that ain't a fool for you; I don't know who 'me' is."

"This is Tole, Penny." His patience was wearing out.

"Tole who?"

"Tole Kirkman, and you can save your damn bullets for your niggers who don't pay for the week on Saturday night."

Penny cracked the door, sticking only her head out and holding her robe shut with one hand. Little silvery sensations crept down his spine. He moved closer, getting a whiff of an oversweet perfume which made his head swim.

"Oh, that's you, Tole. You got off, didn't you?"

"Don't seem to matter none with you," he snapped.

"To tell you the truth, Buster, I don't like the laws near so well as you. I stay outa trouble, and I don't like folks who's always mixed up with 'm."

"Meaning what?" he asked.

"Meaning you come in here and get your goods 'n check."

"So that's the kind you are?"

"No, that's the way it is. I like my fun." She stepped outside of the door, holding the knob with one hand and the robe with the other. "I love fun well as anybody. And I love this town, but I don't want no trouble with no law. Come on in."

"Who you got in there? I know this old act of poking your head out the door and stalling for time asking who knock."

"Nobody in here to hurt you, if you know how to act and if you know how to check." She started taking a cleaner's bag from behind the door.

"I don't have nothing to put no clothes in tonight, honey. Nothing but my hands, sugar plump."

"Should've brought you a suitcase."

"Penny."

"You just lay off my name and just don't be wasting so much time. These your cover-alls and suits. Here's your pajamas and little things in this paper sack."

"So you had me all packed up before I came?"

"If that's the way you want to put it." She smiled as she opened the door to usher him out.

Once under the sky of the early August night, he felt the impact of Penny's sentence more severely than the judge's order to serve on the road for ninety days.

This was the second big lie that had exploded in his face. The first lie was one which had encouraged him to get away from his father's household of twelve and from Old Man Griffin's seventh-grade class to find happiness.

"Man," everybody had said, "if you get yourself a good job making you a lot of money, you can drop them books, and your old man too. Then you can get yourself a good-looking wife what got enough skin and hair to give the children some looks and be happy. After that, get you a woman. And be sure to get you a good boss to keep you out of trouble."

Tole believed this enough to stop school to become a delivery boy for Mr. Crews. He had a motorbike marked CREWS PHARMACY that could take him anywhere he needed to go in the residential section of Wedgefield. He was known as a good delivery boy because he didn't stop by to talk to anyone when he had to make a trip.

Three years later, when he was fifteen, Mr. Crews recommended him as a good boy to work with his friend who had a grocery store. Now he went out with the man in a truck to deliver groceries in Wedgefield and as far out as Dubose Crossing. When they got out of the residential district, the truck driver started teaching him to drive. By the time he was seventeen, he had gotten his driver's license. When he was nineteen, he married Elease Stenson, a cute seventeen-year-old, and rented two rooms of a duplex on South Mary Street. All his father had said was, "Take a blue hen chicken to get up and scratch for her biddies every day." And his mother had responded in her tired voice by saying, "Tole's a smart boy, Titus. You know all my folks work hard. What's in the blood can't be beat out the bones." Elease's people had said only, "You not worrying how the children'll come out that don't take skin and hair atta us."

Youth and the good job saved them from the cares of life for two months. He was a full-time delivery man for Howell's Wholesale Grocery Company, and enjoyed taking Elease with him on longer trips to show her off. They talked and giggled together about a dog fight or any other trivial incident. She kept the two rooms like a showplace. The bedroom was the living room too, and the kitchen served as dining room and bathroom. The porch lavatory was shared by both families, but the other couple was young and competed with the Kirkmans in keeping their part of the premises tidy.

The washtub baths in the kitchen were a special treat. Elease always had Tole's water heated when he arrived. He remembered how his father had had to thunder and threaten his mother in order to get water for his bath. He started bringing ice cream or a cake or candy to Elease on bath nights as a treat for being a thoughtful wife.

At the end of their second month of marriage, she knew she was pregnant. The July sun which set on their side of the house caused their apartment to feel like an oven for the greater part of the night. She became irritable and complaining because she had heard that a pregnant woman was a sick woman and immediately needed extra attention, different food and an exceptional amount of rest. From the day she received the doctor's statement until the day her baby became a month old, her mother paid a visit every day or sent one of her children to check on Elease's condition. If Tole got his bath water only once in a while during this period, he was uncomplaining. If he got one meal a day, he was completely satisfied. He made excuses for the slights he received because of her condition, and felt that things would be different when the baby got on his own feet.

But Junior was a puny baby who cried and kept him in Mr. Crew's drugstore. The trouble with the baby and what her mother said she should do were the only things they talked about. But he loved Elease and the baby, so he worked hard on the job and at home to make the best of his marriage. They stayed in the two rooms until after the fifth baby came. They got a four-room house and three more babies. He could see no end to diapers in the bathroom, diapers drying on the back of kitchen chairs, and in the oven if the weather was bad. He could see no end to diapers and doctors bills or Elease's suffering through each nine-month period of each pregnancy, with no time to comb her hair, or to clean the house. No time to love him. But then, when they loved, it was the making of another baby.

The lie was a gross one. He had a wife and a family, but he was not happy. He had a good job, but he was not able to save one cent. He had been so anxious to leave his father's house to begin his own family, but now he wished that he had not rushed into adult responsibility. The thought occurred to him that neglecting a duty at home now and then would bring some kind of satisfaction. Other men were enjoying themselves at Joe's Place while he walked the floor with his babies.

Mr. Crews had known him since his teen-age years, so he decided to ask for a credit account there for drugs. That way he could have for his own pleasure the money he pretended to pay for the medicine. His first evening at Joe's Place was disgusting — that is, he provoked the seasoned old scoundrels with his bragging and gluttonous drinking bout. Ed Scott pulled him aside later and told him that the men were sure to mark him as an apron-string boy if he didn't know how to be casual about his escapades. He allied himself with Ed's group after the talk, taking cues from Ed on how to proceed until it was his time to set the house up. After this, the men who frequented Joe's Place considered him a brother. He met them faithfully for bull sessions, drinking rounds, card games, and checkers. He was becoming satisfied, which was just as good to him as being happy.

The choice topic became women, and he had nothing to say because he had been a faithful husband. Ed told him that there wasn't any need for him to play pretty with the gang, because all of them were married but all of them had at least one extra.

Ed laughed as he said, "What's for a colored guy who won't write no book, never cross the ocean unless Uncle Sam send him, never have a real holiday — say nothing 'bout a vacation — never be the president or nothing — I say, a fun loving, sweet-smelling mama is about all you got to sparkle you up."

Tole's mouth fell open as Ed talked.

"Just play it cool," he advised Tole. "Just give your extra enough time to keep her happy and enough money to keep her sweet. Just keep her on the tip of your finger. If you squeeze her in the palm of your hand, you're in for trouble."

How to meet a girl was the next problem. He knew that women considered him "a good-looking black nigger" who was tall enough for his clothes to look right on him. And some girls had said all he had to do was to look at them, because his eyes hypnotized them. But he had taken it all lightly in the old days, because his mother had told him that only forward women said such things, and they would not make him a decent wife because they'd tell other men the same things. He remembered that he had never really given his wife a compliment or said outright, "I love you." And she had never once said, "I love you, Tole." But they had agreed, without saying too much, that they liked each other and wanted to make each other happy. Still, he wanted some woman, not Elease — some sweet-smelling mama, to spin in a romantic dream with him.

As he stopped to deliver orders for the wholesale company, he found himself looking around for this woman. He wanted something within himself to leap up and say, "That's her!"

About two months after Ed's conference, it happened. He walked into Counts' Grocery Store to find a set of hazy-brown eyes standing still in the roundest sweet Georgia-brown face that he had ever seen. She just stood there behind the counter with her lips pursed and her right fingers stroking her coal-black hair which hit even to her shoulders. Instead of asking for Mr. or Mrs. Counts, he stood there checking her down to the waistline.

"Thought you brought the stuff in, then checked," she said.

"Pardon?" he asked.

"I thought you delivery men brought the stuff in, then checked the ticket." She began stroking her hair with the left hand. "You delivery guys sure don't worry about no time schedule."

"Look, baby," he slapped the hand which smoothed her hair. "You can make time stop for me, if you know what I mean?"

She backed away from the counter.

"I got my work to do in the house, you know. Mr. Counts had to take his wife to Emergency in the hospital's, why I'm here. So you come on and bring the stuff in."

"He likes to check the sheet, because one time they put the wrong name on the order, so we had to reload a big order," Tole explained.

"Whatever you say."

"Tole Kirkman — just Tole to you, sugar plump."

"I'm Penny, Penny Motts, and business is business. I got my work to do in the house. I'm just getting the order in. I'm closing up soon's the order's in, if it ever get in. And they got telephones in this town now, and a telephone book."

"That's telling me off all right." He smiled and pinched her arm.

He left the order, and did his first bit of reckless driving because he was sure that she was watching from the window as he took off.

When he did find her place in Field Quarters, and when she finally consented to be his girl, he held her, cherishing her, forgetting about Elease and the eight children. Penny got him in her clutches the very first time. He had gotten as drunk as a dog, had even wallowed a few times (he was told); but the liquor was not so strong as that of his new love.

Elease seemed more detestable now than ever, and the children too. Elease, sleeping heavily with mangled hair in a faded gown, never inspired him now to seek her love. The tired little demons piled into several beds suited him best when they were sleeping. He could remember each new baby as something desirable, smelling of baby oil and powder, and something nice to touch and to kiss because they smiled. Some even made dimples. But later they became little pests. They cried too much or ate too much or made too much noise. He had helped to people this jungle, but he swore that he wouldn't endure it.

He could picture the old rose-flowered wallpaper in Penny's

bedroom, and the array of pretty pictures tucked around the wall of trees, birds, flowers and rustic scenes where beautiful girls and their lovers lay in tall, cool grass. He thought of the ice bucket and the service for two on the night table at Penny's house. He was getting a record player for her birthday, and they would have sweet music to go along with that sweet-smelling perfume while they made sweet love.

His reverie was often broken with, "Tole, go take the baby up; she had the fever all day, and you know this was washday for me." Or, "Tole, if you don't bring some more meal or flour when you come back from work, won't be nothing here to feed the children on in the morning." Or a sigh, "Lord help me to live at this poor dying rate."

The sound of Elease's voice came on with laments, and Penny's with pleas. "Daddy, when you going to be all mine? It takes you too long to get here and you leave too early. I can't hold on to you, when you won't let loose."

To please Penny, Tole started staying until an hour before time to go to work. No matter what time he came home, Elease opened the door and fixed whatever she had to cook, even though she fussed until he left. After a while, he would wait until she fixed it, then empty it in the garbage pail. He hoped that she would cry, but she didn't. It would provoke him that she was not passionate enough to demand a showdown by not letting him in or by not fixing his food. Twice he wrecked the truck, and twice his employer paid for the offenses to keep him from serving on the chain gang when he told him frankly that he was having trouble at home.

"Look, Tole," Mr. Howell told him, "why don't you do like the other boys? Get you a girl. Too many women in the world for you to upset yourself. You the best boy I've got. You don't steal, like some I had, so I want to keep you outta trouble. Wisen yourself, then. You're young and got money in your pocket."

With an ally, Tole got bolder. He moved his Sunday clothes

and shoes to Penny's house so that he could spend the whole weekend with her. Then he moved his work clothes and his personal items, going by his house only to leave the rent and money for food and to half-tease the children. Then he came only to leave the money when the children were asleep.

Nothing, nobody, mattered as much as Penny. She made his blood sing and he was happy.

After he had lived with Penny for two months, he decided that he would speed up deliveries so that he could spend an extra hour at home during the noon hour on her day off from work. For one thing, he was hungry — more hungry for food this day than for love. He picked up four pounds of T-bone steaks and planned to have her make some creamed potatoes. He could kick off his shoes and relax, listen to music, eat, then take a nap.

When he came to the house, the blinds were drawn and there was apparently no one stirring. Two glasses on the night stand had been used and a mound of cigarette ashes filled the big tray. There was a platter with particles of food.

"Penny," he called. "Penny."

"For the love of Mike, why you yelling your guts out? I'm right here in the bathroom."

"What you doing in the bathroom this time of day?" he demanded.

"The hell with you!" she retorted. "If you're not the damndest fool I ever met. What the hell's a bathroom for, any time of day? Want me to tell you? I will if your mama forgot to tell you."

"I brought us some good steak to cook, and I want some of those creamed potatoes you make."

"The burners'll turn on for you just like for me. Never saw such a goddamn helpless-assed bull. I'm not your slave, you know. Say, Buster, what you know I don't know? That's interesting, that I'd like to know."

"I'll cut your living throat, that's what I'll do!" He walked to the bathroom door. Tole tried the door, but she had it locked on the inside.

"Open the door, you two-cent hussy. If you don't, I'll break it down."

"You do that," she said, "and they'll only have to clean up the bathroom."

He left the house storming. He was tempted to go back, but decided to lunch at the shop and go back to work. He drove through the Quarters not seeing and not caring. He turned the corner onto the next street and plunged into the back of the Wedgefield Furniture truck.

Judge Moise sat with his broad shoulders heaved frontwise. He was a new judge in the Ville County courthouse, but he was old in the knowledge of rustic fox play. He had no love for Negroes, but he hated the bosses who indulged their boys more than his preacher grandfather had hated female gospel-mongers. He was for law which bore the stamp of moral integrity. And Tole Kirkman, he had been told, had a boss who paid him out of trouble every time he offended the law.

"Make an example outta him," he told the clerk, "and I'll be in or out and be done with it. If it's anything I can't stand, it's a white man playing papa to a niggrah culprit. And I'll be damned if I don't make an end to it or be found trying."

Working through his help down to the janitor, Judge Moise had a "case history" on Tole Kirkman by the date of his trial. Besides, he had baited the trap in an easy way. He called Tole's employer, talked pleasantly and said that he understood that Negro men had to have an extra woman to keep themselves happy. Somehow the word got to Tole that Mr. Howell had fixed things up with the new judge. He decided to make-up with Penny by buying her a new outfit if she promised to come to the trial. She promised, so they were reconciled.

Meanwhile, Judge Moise sent a welfare worker to check on Tole's family. The report strengthened the judge's resolve to execute his plan. He was told that the children were under-nourished and ill taken care of because the mother's health was failing and her operating funds were insufficient. The welfare worker requested Elease to appear with the eight children at the trial at Judge Moise's request.

Tole Kirkman came in dressed in his next-best Sunday clothes and with a new summer straw hat in his hand. Penny looked like a cut-out doll in her new outfit. He sat down calmly, crossed his legs and winked at Penny. He felt for the signed, incomplete check which Mr. Howell had given him with orders to be back to work after lunch. She winked back, smiling carefully, her mouth full of gum which she popped on the slightest provocation.

She almost swallowed her gum as she followed Tole's eyes across the courtroom.

Elease came in with the baby in her arms and all of the others straggling behind her. Junior prodded the smaller ones, getting them all seated in a row just before court was called to order.

"That's them?" Penny asked. He nodded. He felt that Elease was trying to provoke him by coming there, straggling along with all their puny, ill-kept children.

Tole was called to the bench and pleaded guilty, as Mr. Howell had told him to do. He then handed the judge the envelope. He took it, put it on the stand and continued.

"Are you married, Kirkman?"

"Yes, sir."

"I assume you have no children; you seem to be a newly wed."

Tole dropped his head. "In a way," he answered.

"What way?"

"I wouldn't like to talk about no way, because my business up here is about hitting that truck."

"You're right," the judge said. "You're right. You hit the truck, when it had a red flag out in the back."

"I said I was guilty." Tole raised his voice.

"Yes, you're a man against the law because you have two wives, so that makes you a bigamist who goes around smashing up things just like you smash up people. I ought to sentence your other wife, your common wife, right along with you."

"Your sentence is ninety days on the road, and suspension of your driver's license for a year. The Welfare Department will take care of Elease and the children. I'll mail this back to your boss." He waved it.

Neither of the women, no doubt for their separate reasons, visited him on the prison farm.

———

Ten o'clock was not too long after dark, the way time was measured during the summer in Wedgefield. As he walked away from Penny's house in the August night, life was just beginning for the couples who lived for fun and loving. He had been put out, and tried not to care, but the thought of another's taking his place provoked him. A man, a real man, the group would say, would ambush the new guy, or at least shoot him in the foot. A real man would not let another man take his woman without a fight. He wanted Penny's affection, but he did not want to fight for her. He had never really seen another man in her house or leaving it. He wondered if she had devised the trick to test his spunk or to prove her worth by egging him on so that he could divorce his wife, Elease.

The scene with the judge made him think of Elease and the children. That day he was ashamed of her and the children. They had looked the part of the dispossessed that they were, and he hadn't liked it. Elease could have spruced up to keep the other woman from seeming so attractive. She could have styled her hair and put on some lipstick. She had helped to drive him away.

He walked on through the Quarters with his clothes rolled in a tight bundle under his arm. He did not have the money to rent a room for the night, and for the first time in his life he did not know where he would sleep.

"Hell," he said. "I'm going home. That's where I'm going. If that bastard Moise wants to put me in trouble because I took Penny, then damn it to hell, he's not making me work ninety days to wander around in the streets." He thought of saying "Elease, I'm sorry and I want to come back home." Instead he decided to bully her. He'd tell her that he was going to the World's Fair, to Atlantic City, New Jersey, and then on over to the West Coast to visit his brother in Los Angeles. He'd let her know that he was no trash and that he had people in far-away places who stood for something and who cared for him.

He reached 1490 South Mary Street before he had finished mapping out his tour.

He knocked the second time before the light went on.

Elease asked, "Who is it?"

"Me."

"What you want, Tole?" she asked.

"Open the door, woman," he commanded.

She opened the door and stood cautiously in the clearing.

"You're not going to let me in?"

"Why should I let you in?"

"Jesus Christ, a man can't come in his own house?"

"You didn't leave from here, Tole, so you got no right to come stirring me up if she turned you out."

"I just want to talk over something," he said in a casual voice.

"All right, just a minute." She put on a pink-flowered cotton housecoat and a pair of soft pink house-slippers. He noticed that her hair was put up in pink curlers. She had gotten up from a hide-a-way bed that looked clean and comfortable.

"You sick?" he asked. "Nobody slept in here unless they were sick — made it convenient when company called?"

"No, the lady said it was best for the parents not to sleep in the room with the children. I put the girls in the front bedroom and the boys in the back room. If one gets to feeling bad, I take him in here until he feels better."

"I see. Well, I'm going to the World's Fair and to California. Nobody wants to take a wife to California with her hair standing up on the top of her head. And nobody likes baby diapers drying in the stove where you got to cook his bread. It's some things a man won't stand. And he feels like a fool when he wants to disown his own blood. I'm going to California, to Los Angeles, where my brother is, the one who's living like a king."

"Whatever are you raving about?" she asked. "You're your own man. The Welfare is taking care of us. But I said I didn't want to stay on the Welfare. Bad enough for the children with you on the road, and this Penny business, and now people tease them about 'not to be sold.' But they helped, and I had time to get myself together. I'm studying to be a hairdresser."

"You didn't even say you loved me, never did. Every little brat around here rated more than me."

"I can have my shop at home. I'll start in the kitchen, but I'll ask Mr. Jenkins to add two rooms so I can have a bedroom for myself and a room to work in."

"Here I haven't eaten since this morning, and my own wife hasn't offered me a thing to eat. A man'll have to leave the South to find a woman who knows how to treat people."

"Junior's not but ten, but he's a little man. He helps my father gather his vegetables and sell them."

"I used to say we don't talk, but we do. We talk forever. Especially when a man's starving to death in his own home."

"You stop saying that, you hear me. You stop saying that, Tole Kirkman. You left me. Remember. You left me. Go bully your whore." She stood firmly waited for his reply.

"Well, the sickly little saint has got some mule in her at last," he goaded her.

"Call it what you want to; but at the beauty shop, I learned how people act, good and bad, listening to the customers. Both of us were wrong; you worked hard, and I stayed out the street, and that's about all we called our marriage. We had a real nice time for two months; and after I started the family, everything fell to pieces."

"I don't know you," he said, looking at Elease. "I married you, but I didn't know you. I don't now, but you make a lot of sense."

"And I don't know you either. And I didn't know you hated the baby diapers in the oven, because you didn't say so."

"I guess all that's not's hard as a man laboring hard everyday for nothing. Not even eight babies in ten years."

"Did Penny Mott put you out, or did you put her down to come back home?"

"I guess, if she put me out, you don't want me either." He kept his eyes away from her.

"Tole." She stood before him. "I'm not saying I'm right. I have to know the truth."

"She sent me away, Elease. And I'm not going to beg to stay here, either. I need to find myself. I want to be a good father and a good husband, but I'm not sure that I want to scratch everyday."

"I understand," she said.

"You understand that I don't want to miss out on life because of you and the children; that I, me, myself, want to live?"

"Yes, Tole, I didn't know what it was like for one to feel that he had to keep things moving every day, but I got a taste of it when you left. It's not easy. And I've found out that people work together. They go to church, to picnics, to programs and to visit their people, even though they have more children than we've got; and they're not complaining about it, either."

"Jesus Christ, I can't stay in the street all the time, or up in the air, or wherever I've been."

"Don't use the Lord's name in vain, Tole."

"I guess not," he agreed.

They sat, exhausted from the talk. Several minutes passed in silence. After all of the talk, she noticed that Tole still held the rolled cleaner's bag in his arm; he had his hat on, and the smaller bag at his feet.

"Tole," she got up to leave, "rest your hat and hang the bag behind the door in the other room while I fix some bath water for you."

He took his hat off, then his shoes, and walked quietly into the other room.

The Bouncing Game

Aaron shifted his two hundred and thirty-seven pounds from one foot to the other a dozen times before Mr. Dwyer, the oldest teller at the Citizens National Bank, let one word fall.

"No, son, your father just don't have sufficient funds."

The old man leveled his metal-framed spectacles with the point of his index finger, resting them just above the top of his nose. The young man looked wistfully through the teller's cage while the soft flesh quivered on his jaws.

"Mr. Dwyer," Aaron summoned new courage, "I'm asking you about Jutson Spraggs. You know, I just said Spraggs when I asked you to check the mistake about my father's check. You see, I've never known this kind of thing to happen with him."

"My boy, I've been knowing the family all of my life. You're Aaron, Jut's youngest son, eh? The other two —"

"Thank you, Mr. Dwyer."

Aaron walked away — choosing no direction.

"My old man's checks bouncing?" He spoke to himself. "I'll be a gorilla's damn grandpa before I take that."

Aaron stood just outside the door of the bank with his fists crammed in his pockets. A fiendish smile moved over his face.

"Damn old miser."

He left the spot, turning right. As he looked back, the building itself seemed to jeer as he sauntered two blocks farther to the Suffolk Road bus stop.

On boarding the bus, he ignored the people he knew, his ruddy complexion deepening as he thought of his predicament.

In the first place, he had not been interested in paying $39.95 for the set of semi-porcelain dinnerware, "Virginia," tastefully decorated, which his wife had to have. Besides, Berta allowed her relatives from Richmond to talk of "coming down" to Suffolk as if they were coming from Alaska. And she had insisted that a woman married for five years, with two children, should have a whole set of dishes as well as a set of whole dishes.

He lighted a cigarette to abate his mounting anger.

He wondered now how he had let himself be taken in by Berta's craving for dishes. Anyway, he had written a check for the complete sum to Jennings Hardware. He knew that he had less than $5.00 in his checking account. He knew also that his father would save the reputation of the Spraggs family. But his father had come to his aid by writing a check for Mr. Jennings to cover the cost of the dishes when his (Aaron's) check had bounced — and now that check had bounced. The debt remained.

And Mr. Dwyer had stood there stretching his Adam's apple, adjusting his spectacles, and struggling to give a verbal chronicle of the Spraggs ancestry — knowing his dilemma.

The cigarette had not helped. He was still angry.

Now Aaron did not try to abate his anger. As the bus joggled along, he fed his anger by repeating words over and over as he had done as a child to preserve a mood.

"Damn old miser. Damn old miser. Damn old miser."

Jutson Spraggs heaped peanut vines on the new stack. He knew the rattle-rattle of the Suffolk Road bus, as well as the long, screeching halt which announced a visitor. Too often the visitor turned out to be one of his three sons. Almost always the bus stopped when he was on the outside — about his work on the farm. Often he wished that someone would come when he was inside the house, alone.

He threw pile on pile, drinking in the fresh autumn air. He had learned to hate the house, especially on Sunday afternoons.

His thoughts drifted to other days, when he had to measure his footsteps to avoid the appearance of racing when he headed toward the house. He remembered, too, how he, along with the boys, had vied for Anna's hot biscuits and homemade sausage, and the chance to drink from the old brown mug, the only heirloom in the family.

Now, the boys came. And their wives. And the grandchildren. But they came together and stuck together as if he were King Kong, ready to pounce upon them. Then they never came except on Christmas Day, Easter Sunday and Father's Day.

If one of the youngsters chased a rooster, there would be a switching and a lecture about roosters spurring children, maybe piercing an eye. If the little feet pattered loud enough to be heard, there was the everlasting "Sh-sh-sh," or "Don't disturb Grandpa."

No. He did not relish the visits. Or the sons, or their families.

The stack was well above his shoulders now.

"Hi, Pa."

Jutson stopped in his tracks. He had never known the bus to stop during the day without his hearing it.

Slowly he turned around to face his youngest, "healthiest," most extravagant son. Twenty-six years, two hundred pounds of worthlessness, he thought.

"Nice work you're doing there, Pa."

Jutson reached for his pipe, filling and lighting it without replying. He stood a moment longer, adjusting his old brown hat (now a nameless gray), which flapped comfortably toward his face.

"Guess it's about time I get busy, since frost is due soon." Jutson started another pile of vines.

Aaron did not know how to cope with the change. He had waited for the usual scolding: "You're a worthless scoundrel, working harder than your brothers to ruin the family name," or "You take this money and get off my premises as fast as you can."

But this.

"How's Berta Mae and the children? Did she tie that mole's foot in that sack around the baby's neck? He surely will teethe easy."

Aaron shifted his position for the first time.

"Boy, you could be in the house. Don't mind me and what I'm doing."

Jutson continued to heap the vines on the new stack as he puffed on his pipe.

Aaron knew the feeling. The way his father had looked at him when he, after deciding to elope, had to tell his secret for lack of money to buy a marriage license.

Aaron moved closer to his father, the desire to give him a left to the chin uppermost in his mind.

"Pa."

The two men faced each other. They stared as if they had never met before.

"Pa," Aaron could play the game no longer. "You know good and darn well what I'm here for, and you putter around here like you're so interested in everything but what I came here for."

"Well now, if you're here for something, you ought to state as much. You just dropped by." Jutson turned to the stack again.

"You know women, Pa. You know how they like to show off. It's a lot of bunk, but they like to show off. Berta just had to have those dishes."

"Yes, women like to show off."

"Look, Pa, I'm a man with a wife and two children, so you've got no right to belittle me."

"And you've got no right coming here on a morning, loitering around while I'm trying to work. You mind, too, because I'm the same number of years above you."

"If you're so awfully mighty, why don't you have some money in the bank, as much as you pinch pennies? Old Man Dwyer'll have the news all over town before noon about your check bouncing."

Again the two men eyed each other.

"Aaron," Jutson found a fatherly tone, "tell me this. When did you start thinking about our reputation?"

Aaron blinked his eyes; his father seemed taller and larger standing there, and it bothered him.

"Pa, the check you gave me for $39.95 bounced."

"Yeah."

"Well, what do I do?"

"I'll have to think." Jutson just stood there.

The old anger began to creep back, but Aaron began to realize that he was the offender. He had come to his father over the years: parking tickets, passing on hills, unpaid grocery bills, unpaid medical fees — and always he had been able to "soak his pa."

Jutson stood there looking at his laziest, "healthiest," most extravagant son, fighting to keep his resolve. He knew that if he had had the grit to stand up to his boys when they were boys, they might now stand up as men. He wanted so much to unroll the bundle of greenbacks which he would redeposit in the Citizens National Bank, but instead he pushed the tilt of the old brown hat away from his face.

"Boy, you're in a pickle. You know you got your own self in it, though. Look — I'll be in town this evening. No — maybe sometimes tomorrow — and I'll talk with Mr. Jennings."

The old happiness returned. Aaron knew that his father had a warm spot which would gradually melt. "The old miser just needs handling, and that I can do," he mused to himself. He began to smile.

"Don't you hear me?"

"Oh, yes sir."

"I don't want the frost to catch these peanuts unstacked. I'm paying $40.00 a week."

"You mean . . ." Aaron's heart sank.

"What must I tell the man?"

Jutson waited for his son to answer.

"Oh Pa, you know me."

"Yeah."

"You know how to talk with him better than I do."

"Yeah. Well, I'll be going to town tomorrow, I guess —"

Again the two men eyed each other as strangers. Jutson broke the spell.

"Boy, there's coffee on the stove if you want some before you start."

Aaron stood still a minute longer, watching his father heaving vine on vine while the stack climbed. He completed his smile.

"I guess so, Pa," he moved toward the house, "since I can have the old mug."

A letter from home departing from the routine of cataloging the new babies, the new funerals or the new weddings was a relic. It did not matter if Mama, Daddy or one of the other children above the fifth grade answered my letter, it almost always said the same thing:

> Just a few lines to let you hear from me. How are you at this time? Fine I hope. Received your kind and loving letter. Hope when these few lines reach your loving hands will find you enjoying the best of life and health.
>
> We know that you need more but things are tight here in Wedgefield. I couldn't send as much money as you needed but I want you to try and make out. We can't complain because many more are in a worse shape than us.
>
> Take care of yourself and don't worry so your grades can be good.
>
> I'll close this letter but not my love.

But the letter which I received from home on Monday, October 13, 1941, was different. My little brother, Bay Boy, had run away to join the Navy.

This letter deserved a special explanation, but unfortunately, no details were given. I wrote several letters, using the precious few pennies that I could ill afford, to find out how and why Bay Boy became interested in Uncle Sam's Navy.

No answer came.

By now I began to wonder how he had fared on leaving. I only wished that I had been at home when he left. I would have fixed a shoe-box lunch of fried chicken, light bread, oranges, apples, bananas, parched peanuts, and squares of light-colored fudge — Bay Boy didn't particularly like cake or pie. I knew that nothing gave a traveler from Wedgefield more joy

Dear Sis

than the shoe-box lunch. Some people wrapped the box as if it were a gift, fancied up with ribbons, but everyone knew the secret.

I studied my books as well as I could under the circumstances, but I could not forget Bay Boy, a tender-skinned boy of sixteen, who had known only the meanest corner of Wedgefield (a town not even on the map) before making this venture. He had been considered as the funny one at home because he talked little, asked for nothing, protested nothing. When he became ill — no matter how ill — he wanted to be left alone.

But Bay Boy was now in the Navy, and they said it was a man's Navy and he was only a boy. How could he have made up his mind to join that man's Navy? He was the only one in our family of eleven, ranging in age from seven to twenty-nine, who had never spent a night away from home. But even so, no one cared enough to tell me about Bay Boy's venture.

———

Time moved on. The war in Europe raged. I found relief in the communal *sanctum sanctorum*: The prayers for peace, the rightful greatness of "God Bless America," the final promise of the parting G.I. voiced even by a three-year-old singing prodigy of the local network: "I'll be back in a year, little darling. Uncle Sam has called and I must go."

At King's College, war was something for me to read about in the newspapers. I had to read the news because ten of the questions out of twenty-five on the semester examination in my Modern European History course were based on current events. I was always prepared to tell Mr. Levant what happened here or there on this date or the other. Sunday afternoon was the only time for actually listening to the news.

On December 7, in the afternoon — I never kept up with the hours on a Sunday afternoon at King's College, for all of the afternoons were one long, solitary hour, with boredom pressing the tips of your elbows as you poured over noble subjects that would make you the world of tomorrow — someone yelled: "The President! The President! The President!"

I could hear feet everywhere.

"Who? President Stone?" someone asked to no one in particular.

"No, fool," someone answered no one in particular. "What's Prexy doing in a girls' dorm on Sunday afternoon?"

"Who?"

Someone snatched my arm as I moved on with the others to Susy Beth's room. And the voice of FDR: "Friends, and you are my friends." The words were spoken with quiet detachment. "I now declare the United States of America in a state of war with Japan."

The war cloud settled over the group of girls huddled in Susy Beth's room. Surely, then, I knew that God must bless America. Bay Boy was somewhere — a part of the Navy. He never even read the news. He was just a boy of sixteen who could get into all kinds of devilment after dark. But now he would have to fight for his country.

The holiday season began on the twentieth of December. I would celebrate Christmas with the family. I would also find out more about Bay Boy's venture.

My hopes rose skyward as the train neared Wedgefield. The wee station, scarcely more than a covered shed to shield the baggage and the few passengers from the elements, was seldom a cheerful place at train time. Knowing that Daddy or Buddy would meet the train relieved me of the fear of carrying my suitcase the whole country mile to the house.

No one met me.

Day had almost come, but enough of the grayness from dawn

tarried to make things some distance away indistinguishable. I could not leave my bag under the shed, so I began walking the mile, changing the suitcase from one hand to the other.

The house was dead.

On being admitted, I found the air rife with those before-arising fumes which, along with the cold pot-bellied heater, said everything but "Welcome home." When I kissed Mama, she gave her typical greeting: "Your nose sure is cold. I thought that the college didn't close until day after tomorrow." And Daddy said "Why didn't you tell us to meet you?"

I moved on toward the mantle, where my letter lay half-opened — the one which I had written telling them when to meet me.

"Where's Bay Boy?"

"A dirty rascal. He sent a dry letter here, his civilian clothes and six pictures. I bet those pictures cost ten dollars. That money could've bought enough groceries for a week."

"Where's Bay Boy, Daddy? I want to see the pictures."

"No need to bother, they're not so good. Looks to me he's scared to death — trying to back away from something."

"Where are they?"

"Muttah, where's Bay Boy?"

"They're on the mantlepiece, behind the clock, I think."

I found the packet.

Here was my brother, standing tall, but without strength. They were signed, every single picture: "All my love, Henry Lee Mingo."

You could not say that he was handsome. He was just a tall, good-looking ginger-colored boy with the typical Booker T. Washington look. He stood between two tall white columns, with his arms dangling to his sides. The sailor suit became him very well, only he stood with his legs far apart, with one foot before the other, as if he were going to walk away as the photographer snapped the pictures.

I looked so long at the pictures, until Daddy called.

"Sugar pie."

"Yes, sir."

"Did I tell you that he sent a dry letter. I know that he must have gotten one paycheck by now."

"Yes, sir."

"When I was his age, I was supporting myself, Grandma and Grandpa."

"Yes, sir."

"You making fire."

"Yes, sir."

"Time for the house to stir."

I looked at the return address on Bay Boy's letter: c/o A.P.O., San Francisco, California.

I would write him on returning to King's College, hoping that he might account for his sudden interest in joining the Navy.

February brought a letter from Bay Boy. I received it in the morning mail, but I would not open the letter until after supper, after I had studied all of my assignments for the next day. It was one of several letters which answered my question: Why?

February 5, 1942

Dear Sis,

I received your kind and loving letter and was very glad to hear from you. I am glad that you wrote first because I thought that you would be mad at me also for leaving school. I guess I let everybody down because they wanted me to finish school and be a great man. Right now I don't know about anything.

I'm just glad you wrote. Now I want to tell you that I cry every night because I wish I had stayed in school. I am only sixteen, as you know, so Daddy didn't have to sign the papers.

One day me and Knocker and Buster got in a little trouble

at school. Mr. Hasty sent us to the Home Ec room to hang up
some drapes. We pulled up one of those long shiny tables to
reach high enough. Well a girl started calling Miss Jenkins from
the kitchen side to show her how we scratched up the serving
table with our shoes. Knocker hauled off and slapped the girl
so we left before that lady got out of the kitchen.

Mr. Hasty said he was going to turn us over to the principal.
I knew that it was going to be rough because my homeroom
teacher knows Miss Janie. You remember I was in her class
when Mama turned me over to the truant officer for playing
hooky when I was in the seventh grade.

(I'm writing the other part a little later.)

But Sis, I didn't even want to play hooky. I had to slip around
the schoolhouse and hide in the toilet. I was glad when they
made me go to class because I didn't know what to do. But old
Beebee used to pick at me every time I put on those blue pants
Mama bought me for Field Day. He started calling me Boy
Blue and the children used to point at me and laugh.

One day I went to the board to work my example and he
pointed at me and said "Boy Blue" and all of the children
laughed. Miss Janie was checking papers and didn't know why
they were laughing.

Oh, what I was saying now about us was that we slipped on
off the school ground when the children were marching to
chapel because we knew the principal was going to call us to
the office. You know how mean Prof. Graham can act. He'd have
sent us home for good. We just went on to the highway and
thumbed on over to Lynchburg to be examined.

(Here we go again.)

I was scared to death but all three of us went on the West
End and bummed around Buster's house until the man from
Lynchburg wrote to say whether or not we passed for the Navy.

I was the only one who passed.

When Daddy got the papers in the mail, he called me a dirty scoundrel and said if I was man enough to walk off and sign up without asking him he was man enough to sign up for me to go.

So I hope this is enough to tell you how I got in the navy. But I wish I was in school now. 10 B wasn't so bad after all.

Write soon to let me hear from you.

Your brother as ever,

Henry Lee

March 10, 1942

Dear Sis,

Just a few lines to let you hear from me. I am well and hope you are the same. I didn't know that you get lonesome in college too. Daddy used to say that college was a great place to be.

I started to say you ought not to cry when you don't get a letter from home, but I guess you said that to let me know that I wasn't the only cry baby in the family. Anyway, Sis, don't let nobody see you crying.

That's right, you asked me if I miss Knocker and Buster. You know I do. It's so funny. No it's not so funny. We used to swear that we would always stay together until we married.

You know what we used to do with the money we got selling junk to Dirty Red? We used to see the same movie three times so that we could learn some of the parts. Mama used to fuss anyway so I just went right on asking to study with Knocker. She thought I wanted to talk to Knocker's sister but I wasn't thinking about that girl. She was a blabber mouth.

If we had hung around Knocker's house like we did at Buster's, she would've told everybody.

Look I'm going to send you some money to get yourself an Easter dress. I guess those girls at King's College have some fine clothes.

Tell me some more about the teacher who jumps up on the desk when he starts teaching his class. I sure would like to see that.

That's right, send me a picture of yourself in the next letter. Some of the fellows don't get any mail so they like to hear the rest of us talk about our letters and look at the pictures that we get.

I will close my letter but not my love.

Your brother as ever,

Henry Lee

April 20, 1942

Dear Sis,

That picture is tops. These fellows sure went on when I showed it to them. They say you look like you're going to be a teacher. (Smile)

I like the dress you bought with the money I sent you. They told me that you looked more like sweet sixteen than I do. Did I do wrong by telling them you were twenty?

What I was trying to prove is that you look swell and that you are smart because you're second year in college. I told them that you could even stop and teach after two years and that would make you a school teacher at twenty. A white fellow from Alabama said that he didn't know that colored girls went to college. He was really surprised to see that campus you sent me with all of those girls doing so many wonderful things.

(Stops for the present time.)

Sis, it's sort of hard for me to tell you a tale. Buddy is between us, but we seem to be a little closer though he's next to me. Anyway here's the real dope. I didn't enjoy my trip from Wedgefield to Norfolk. (I'm too old to tell a tale anyway.)

You write back and tell me if you think it's wrong for me to talk about Mama and Daddy. You know Reverend Short used to say you're supposed to honor your mother and father. You know I don't want a curse to fall on me.

Remember when Sonny and Little Pop got drowned down at the pond? Knocker said they had sassed their grandmother. She shook her dog finger after them and said they would have bad luck.

Well, write back soon and tell me what I asked you.

Say hello to all of your friends and send some pictures of the school or any of your friends when you can.

Your brother as ever,

Henry Lee

P.S. I have not had a letter from Mama yet written in her own hand writing.

May 19, 1942

Dear Sis,

Thanks for the pictures of the school. It's funny, I didn't know that there was a college that looked that good in South Carolina either. When I get back, I want to go to Charlestown, Fort Jackson and all those interesting places that the fellows ask me about.

Now about the trip from Wedgefield to Norfolk. Well, I left home almost seven o'clock, the ninth of October. It was sort of cool so I wore my navy blue Sunday suit and put a sweater underneath it. I had heard that there was a lot of water about Norfolk so I wanted to be warm.

Mama got up to cook some breakfast but it wasn't done by the time I got dressed, so I walked on so the bus wouldn't leave me.

I never did spend a night away from home so I felt funny. When I left I told Mama goodbye, but she was busy. I wanted to look back to see if she was in the door, but I wouldn't. I thought I was going to be glad so I wouldn't hear her fuss no more, but I just felt funny.

I went on by the store to see Daddy. He told me how he had done for all of us from the time Granny came on. He told me to never forget that whenever I wanted to throw my money away. He told me to keep myself clean and then he looked at me a long time.

I wanted to touch Daddy. I got the strangest idea that he wanted to touch me too. But we never did. You know I hadn't touched him excepting when he whipped me since I stopped riding Pete and Tom (Daddy's knees — remember?) (You're used to this now.)

I got on the bus about five minutes after seven on a Thursday morning and it was way up in the morning on Friday when I got to Norfolk. I ate the peanuts I got from the store at the bus station and bought a cold drink. When I got to Charlotte, North Carolina, I had spent my quarter. Right then I wished I was back in South Carolina. I could see something in Wedgefield every time I shut my eyes. And I shut them a lot whether I was asleep or not to forget about being hungry. One lady wanted to give me some of her food but I was not used to eating other people's cooking. I was sort of shame too.

Sis, getting in, you know what I mean, is another story.

All I wish is that Mama and Daddy had asked me "why." If they had, I'd have told them. But they never did ask me why

I played hooky or why I came home so late or why me and Knocker and Buster ran away from school to try to get in the navy.

I wonder why they never asked me "why," Sis?

I hope that you will pass your examinations and have a safe trip back to Wedgefield.

Your brother as ever,

Henry Lee

The Entertainers

> . . . Curious kinks of the human mind . . . cannot
> be laughed away, nor always successfully stormed at,
> nor easily abolished by act of legislature.
>
> —Du Bois

It was mid-morning of a June day when I boarded the Elm Road Bus on the corner of Main and Herbert Drive. The mounting heat seemed to have leveled all existence to sheer endurance. And the passengers: Vacation Bible School teachers with shopping bags stacked with rolls of cardboard and crepe paper; domestic workers, a few giving away the secret by wearing the true-blue uniforms trimmed in white; men with khaki uniforms, some unpressed, some half-clean even on a Monday morning; others tidy enough, with that dead-pan expression or grimace — resigning themselves to a joyless ride, just sat as the bus rattled along.

We passed several stops going on toward town without picking up a single passenger. When we reached the Cedar Drive stop, a gang of new passengers boarded the bus. That's when Cousin Willie and Cousin Annie (not my cousins, but cousins to each other) boarded the bus. When they found seats, each on the center aisle near the front of the bus, the listlessness gave way to an unrehearsed performance. They talked away, catching up on family welfare, present employment — everything. They talked as if the other passengers were not there at all.

Cousin Willie began, after exclaiming over the surprise meeting, to ask Cousin Annie about her present living quarters:

"Annie, where you living now?"

The woman faltered, gave her answer, yet refused to answer the question.

"Well, Cousin Willie, it don't really matter where I live.

Anywhere I live is all right to me, 'cause I got a home up above."

"I mean —"

"You know these white folks not goin' to let you live nowhere too long if you can't keep the rent jam up."

"I just asked," Cousin Willie lowered his voice, "because I'm goin' back home. I'm itching for the smell of the country."

"Oh, well." Cousin Annie let out a ton of breath. "I don't know about me and the country, not any more. I had so many ups and downs out there on the farm. Here in town I catch a little job here and yonder."

"But at my age, Annie, I'm passing the time catchin' a job here and yonder. Though you may have the truth in what you say." The old man looked straight ahead.

"I used to wanta stop payin' taxes on that piece of land out there we all owned over the river, but it got wooded fast and there's plenty of game which make it worth its keeps. I can clear away a spot and build me a little nook for little or nothin'; I can stay there till I shut these eyes for good. I don't want money no more — that's none to speak of. I just want a little peace now and then. That oldest boy o' mine in Dallas has got good money; he won't let me perish nohow."

"If you goin to do that Cousin Willie, I 'spect it's all right. But me, I don't won't to go back, cause ain't no gas or 'lectric out there."

"Now you know, Annie, you can get anything in the rural that you got in town."

Cousin Annie "humphed" real loud. "How you gonna get such in the rural with no money — same as how you gonna keep it on with no money in town?"

"You right, you're sure right, Annie."

But the little brown woman with the tight-pinched chin and fiery eyes would not let the matter rest.

"I still say, if you don't have no money and the white folks don't wantcha where you wanta be, whatcha to do then? You ain't nowhere no way." She "humphed" again.

"Cousin Annie, you right, all right, but when I was out there on Davis plantation, I had some of the best white folks there was. I could take up anything from the store I cared for till the crops was made."

"That's where we differ."

The woman's eyes danced. She shuffled on her half of the seat, trying (seemingly) to find a cool spot.

"Old Man Marcelle didn't mind that neither. It goes as good white folks goes in Louisiana. No. He didn't mind us taking up things at the store. He didn' mind doin' a whole heap o' good for the colored folks till he married that old hellcat from Natchez."

"Mind your mouth, Annie."

"You just hush, Cousin Willie. You listen to me. When she commence' clerkin' in the store, she didn't let nobody pile up on the credit. After the crop was put in, she commence' drawing up the credit."

"I thought she was a right good woman."

"You didn' live out there, neither. I had to leave that place with seven head of childrens in July. You hear me? July! I had to leave!"

Cousin Annie's shrill voice settled over the passengers, all colored passengers, even a colored bus driver, like the benediction of a murderer's funeral rites. No one spoke. No one yawned. No one passed signifying glances. No one made half apologetic or cryptic remarks to counteract the prattle of a less sane member of the group.

The rattle-rattle of the bus was the only sound for a while And as the Wedding Guest felt constrained to hear the tale of the Ancient Mariner to the end, so did the audience listen to the two cousins, the shrill voice and then the level tone.

"Who don't get tired of folks treatin' you like dirt? Just like you ain't no grown person, and just like you ain't got one iota of sense. Humph! I showed them. I took myself off that place quicker than Pat got out of the Army."

"I didn't know that, Cousin Annie."

"It's a whole lot you don't know, Cousin Willie, or either you don't wanta know. But I tell you this: If Bud had been livin', old Lloyd Marcelle woulda found hisself washed in his own blood."

"Now, now, Annie, if you had just come over to my house and told me you were having trouble at Mr. Marcelle before you whipped his wife, I coulda talked to him."

"Was'n' so much trouble as that, Cousin Willie. She was mostly shame 'cause I whipped her fanny all over her own store 'fore all her friends when she tried to show out on me. She just pushed the old man up to make me move 'cause it embarrass' the fool out of her."

"But look —"

"Ain't no 'buts,' Cousin Willie. My baby was one month old and my knee boy was eleven months old. Hoot was just turnin' thirteen."

"That's the oldest one?"

"Yes, Lord."

At this point Cousin Willie tried to change the conversation. "What ever happened to Old Man Marcelle?"

"God is a just God, Cousin Willie. I tell you that. He got trampled in the cow lot so bad till his eyes was knocked out. Further on, his brains become rattled."

"Um-hum."

The bus came to a halt for the Oak Drive stop.

"Is this the last stop before yours, Cousin Willie?"

"No. Two more."

"Well, let me hasten to tell you this before you get off. When I heard of the calamity, I was so glad that I didn' know what to do. I hated him and that old hell-cat of a wife so much, I was wishin' the cows hadda killed them both outright."

Cousin Willie blinked. He turned around in his seat and just looked across the aisle at Cousin Annie.

"Annie, did you hate them that bad?"

"Yes, Cousin Willie, I won't lie. I hated them worse than I said. Lord knows, I hadda right to hate them."

"Annie —"

"In July, Cousin Willie, corn's gettin' grown, green peas, butter beans, okra and such's just right for the pot. Watermelons and cantalopes ready for eatin'. Cotton's not awfully far from pickin'— and somebody throwin' a woman and seven children off a place, and I don't think I hate them. Humph!"

"Annie, you listen to me now. It's no matter you're my cousin, you're just wrong. Don't you know God made every human? He made some white, some black, some red, some yellow and some brown. You hear me? And he didn't make them all the same."

"Brother, you're runnin' off at the mouth, but you didn' move away from Mr. Marcelle in July."

"Now, it hurts me to know that you were treated that way. But all of your children are grown now. You still blessed with health and strength. And none of you-all starved to death even if you did leave the crop. If I was you, I wouldn't hate them."

The entrenched wrinkles across the woman's forehead, formed from habitual frowning, stood out in little separate rows. She looked across the aisle once more and formed a stingy smile as she met the old man's eyes. She took in the close-shaven face of the sturdy black man, well over sixty-five, who held her attention a few minutes. She took in the navy-blue Sunday suit and the not-too-fresh starched white shirt opened at the collar. Before she could speak, after giving him the who-in-the-hell-you-think-you-are glance, the bus pulled up at the curve.

He touched Cousin Annie's shoulder after getting up.

"You take care now. And I wouldn't hate them."

She started to speak, her mouth gaped. No sound came. She knew that he would never understand her viewpoint.

"Must you?" he asked, shaking his head.

Cousin Willie's feet hit the ground before Cousin Annie found her voice again.

The entertainment ended.

Home X and Me

This is the way it was done then — what we call "guidance" and "counseling" now — down our way. Someone who saw something in you walked up and asked, "what you want to be?" And you told him if you were a girl, that you wanted to be a teacher or a nurse. If you were a boy, you said a lawyer, a preacher or a doctor. After this you proceeded — just proceeded.

With good fortune, I harbored a boon that would insure my choice of vocation, in addition to the Question. I had an older sister who was two grades ahead of me. When I reached the fourth grade, I began to welcome her intention to "learn" me the choice assignments that the teachers "learned" her. For instance, everyone in the school knew that Miss Daisy (as I'll call her) required the sixth-graders to recite: "I sigh for the land of the cypress and the pine, where the jessamine blooms and the gay woodbine." Instead of reciting a wise saying like "Good, Better, Best" during morning devotions, I lorded my prestige over the fourth-graders by saying all of "The Cypress and the Pine."

This pattern persisted. When I was in fifth grade, my sister had to work the "good and bad road problems" in the seventh grade. I worked them too. When I was in sixth, she was in eighth, 'way on the other side of the track, in high school. That's when she began stuffing my head with Home X. She knew how to cream the butter, how to make white icing stay on a cake, and how to make shredded coconut stay on the white icing. So I didn't bat an eye (I had no cause to) when my seventh-grade teacher handed me my promotion card and asked the Question. I spoke right up and said: "I want to be a Home X school-teacher." She smiled and patted me on the back, being intelligent enough to know, I thought, that I was more than ready to proceed.

Three months later, one never-to-be forgotten September morning in 1934, I left my homeroom class for the Home X building. But they didn't have it spelled the way my sister called it, over the entrance arch. I didn't have time to write down what they had up there, because the crowd shoved me along too fast. I was inside a spacious room with scores of sleek-surfaced oblong tables, with chairs all around them, before I could walk independently. I had never seen a schoolroom without desks. In fact, I had never seen a room like this one before. We huddled in little-girl clusters for security while the teacher waved her arms as if she were lashing at mosquitoes.

"Girls! Girls! Girls! My, my." She held one side of her face as if she had the toothache. "Sit down at the tables." She whisked through the narrow passes between the tables, dropping a neat stack of paper slips on each table. "Last name first; first name second; middle name last."

We sat there like victims of battle fatigue, not rallying at all to what she had just barked out.

"For heaven's sake, I'm asking each of you to write your own name. Can't you do that?" She sat on the corner of the desk, waiting.

"How you want us to write it?" a girl asked.

"Listen — no, I'll write on the board." She wrote a name on the board.

"Is that your name?" another girl asked.

"Yes," the teacher replied. "And now, may I give you the requirements for this course?"

"Yes ma'am," someone answered.

She shook her head, then told us what to expect — a notebook being one of the more important demands.

She made a smile, then read from a small notebook with checkered design: "Food is any substance —"

We sat with undivided attention.

"Girls, please open your notebooks. When I begin dictating again, I want you to write it down. Let me begin again," she said. "Food is any substance which, when taken into the body, is capable of one or more of the following functions: First, building and repairing tissues —"

I could scarcely hold my peace. What was this woman up to? I asked myself. I'd wanted to learn more about making good cakes. And she stood there, all prim and cool and tall, laughing with her medium-brown eyes, and passing her hand over her straightened slick bob, never caring at all about creaming the butter. That's what I wanted to do. That's why I had chosen Home X as my vocation.

"Building and repairing tissues," she had said. Who'd ever heard of food doing that? When we ate at home, we didn't eat to build or repair anything. We ate to fill our stomachs. Where had she been? Where had she come from, not to know what food was really for?

A girl raised her hand, breaking the spell.

"What was the last thing that you said?" she frowned.

"Building — building — building" — her proud square nose was wrinkling as she spoke. "If I'm not mistaken — line up! Come by the desk with an armpit set to meet my nostrils. 'Mum' is the word. They sell it; you buy it; you use it." She sat down for the sniffing exercise.

"Never fear," my heart whispered as it bumped, sounding like raps on a big bass drum. "You cleaned your body with care."

And I had. I had scrubbed carefully with warm water and octagon soap. I had deodorized my armpits with Arm and Hammer baking soap to be sure. I had sprinkled a little between my toes to keep my brown oxfords sanitary on the inside. So there had been nothing else that I knew of that a thirteen-year-old could have done to make herself dainty.

I marched along, hearing my father's voice, and finding comfort in the sound: "Et too, brew tay." He had told us that that was all a man could say when he found out that his best friend had helped to stab him to death. This lady was the one to help me be what I wanted to be. Already she had become Enemy Number One. There was nothing to say but "Et too, brew tay," as my father said when someone he liked pushed him to the wall.

"No one?" she said, after sniffing thirty-four armpits. "Maybe someone slipped out." She counted the slips on the desk. "Yes, thirty-five. But don't get happy, I'll catch her if she stays in this class. Believe me. In the name of health and sanitation, I mean for you to look clean, be clean and smell clean."

On and on the password was "Mum." "Mum" was the password as we took notes on "food" for three weeks, as we worked three weeks on our kitchen outfits, and as we went to the kitchen to learn to cook.

Cooking was my hope for realizing the joys of Home X. The kitchen, with its peculiarities, caused me to wonder if I would succeed after our first briefing. For one thing, the stove cooked with gas. Before anyone could ask a question about what the teacher had said, she looked at me and said sweetly, "You light the oven." I turned the gas on, scratched a match as she had done (because the pilot wasn't working), and applied it underneath. I lost my eyelashes, my eyebrows, a half inch of hair from the line and a week from school to soothe my face from the blown heat with cocoa butter.

Just before the end of the first nine-week period, the teacher announced that we would make lemon meringue pies for the Superintendent and Members of the Board of Education, who always dined in the Department of Home Economics after the official annual meeting. A crew of thirty-six, including the teacher, turned out the day before the visit, in white starched cooking aprons and headbands, to make a dozen pies. I looked around feeling pride, even joy, on being one of this group. I stood there dreaming of the beautiful pies we'd make.

"Get the lemon squeezer. Don't just stand there. Get the lemon squeezer, I said! I mean you, Jackson!" The teacher stood akimbo, her dark skin darkening even more as I froze. "I guess you don't know where to find it. All right. It's in the other room."

Thirty-five spotlights hit me as I turned to fetch that lemon squeezer.

Once I reached the dining room, I felt relief because a ninth-grader was in there polishing the table.

"Where's the lemon squeezer?" I asked her.

"Lemon squeezer?" She loud-talked me. "You tell me, girl, you don't know a lemon squeezer when you see it?"

The teacher heard her and picked up on the cue. "Ah, hah! You were going to fool me. You don't know what a lemon squeezer is. Ah, hah!"

I cowered in the other room as another member of the cooking class got the lemon squeezer.

"Thank you, dear." She used her best speaking voice. "Girls," she continued, "you ought to pay attention to what your mothers teach you."

"Pay attention." I had to pay attention and adhere to *my* mother's teachings, just as she had been taught to obey *her* mother. There had been generations of obedience, but neither mother would have recognized a lemon squeezer had it been the size of one of the modern football bowls.

Even though embarrassment stung me regularly because of a previous lack in homemaking knowledge and skills, I took Home Economics for four years, learning mostly what Negro women on my side of the track couldn't know. And though I knew that me and Home X had parted company as lifelong mates the very minute I left the other room, I have never stopped thinking of the teacher as the emancipator who helped us to become American women.

Lost Note

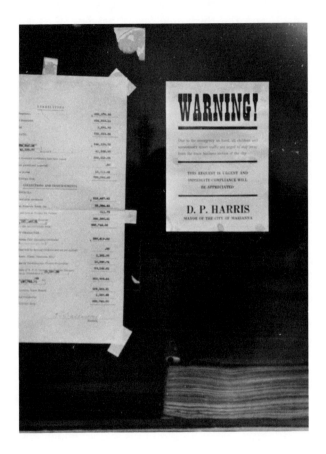

Autumn in the South is a season shouting with joy.

It is a time for reaping what has been sown earlier. It is the time that marks the end of vigorous labor in the vast cotton fields and the thick sugar-cane patches. It is a time for selling and buying, of swapping small talk and big lies in the marketplaces.

It is the time of the County Fair, where tons of sizzling delicious, half-clean, foot-long hot dogs are devoured by the shoveling, amiable prize-seekers.

It is the time for airing classrooms for the anxious new members.

With this autumn, however, a heavy grief came to mar the expected happiness of the season.

The men in the marketplaces talked about it instead of their profits. The housewives abandoned the fence conferences for long sit-down talks.

When the news reached her town, Clara Atkins denounced God momentarily for creating black men. Then she asked God to forgive her for the wicked thought. She tried to sleep to avoid thinking, but even a light nap conjured up the image she wanted to close from her mind.

In her dream, a policeman with a beet-red face harrassed her by jerking her closer to a huge fish net tangled over the body of a boy she imagined to be her grandson.

As soon as the school children cleared the street the next morning, she crossed the street to Nursery Belle McCants' house.

"Nursey," she called, "where you?"

Clara sat down in the porch swing, which was almost hidden from the street by a thatch of ivy vines.

She stung Nursey McCants with the question as soon as she settled herself in the swing.

"I came to ask you how Juny Boy taking it?"

"I 'druther not speak of it, Clara."

"Me neither, Nursey, but we got to do something whether we want to or not. Both of us is fading widow women (I'm in my fifty-nine) with a young boy, a piece we didn't ask for. But by the mercy of the Lord, we got them, and they all we got."

"You speak the truth, Clara, but ain't no guarantee we going to keep them because we got them."

"You're right Nursey," she said, "but I can't see nothing happening here in Wedgefield like it happened across yonder in Mississippi River country. I don't know the answer any more, though, to tell the truth."

"Clara, in my whole sixty-two-odd years here, I ain't never known no big trouble to come between them and us."

"No, Nursey, but since they fished that child out the river over yonder, the air is tight about town."

"I been on pins, too, Clara. But look at all the people over the world who don't like it."

"I'm glad to see who don't like it, but none of that won't bring him back, Nursey. None of it."

"What we to do, Clara? I pray until I get shame bothering the Lord."

"We got to ram some sense in these boys' heads."

"Since Juny Boy made twelve, I can talk to him a little more. That's all I can do, Clara."

"Well, I can't say that for Son. Something's left out of his middle. You don't tell me something ain't wrong with a boy that sleeps through frying bacon and perking coffee every morning."

"Maybe he just can't smell, Clara."

"That's just what I'm trying to get at. He don't use all of his senses."

"Don't you ever talk out your mouth — just tell him down to a tittle?"

"You know I do, Nursey, but as hard as I try to teach him manners, he goes telling the wrong folks 'yes' and 'no.' Besides, he whistles when he gets good and ready to, in season and outa reason. And so far, I can't stop that."

"You don't like for me to say it, Clara, but Son's bound to have some of that up-the-road blood in him from his mama's side."

"Whatever he's got in him, he needs something else. He hasn't got that something to make you love or hate a lot. He hasn't got that something that makes you smell trouble a mile off."

"Juny Boy's got a lot of that in him from somebody, if not me."

"Well, since Son hasn't it, Nursey, I got to help give it to him so as my coat skirt'll be clear from here to Glory."

She stood waiting for Nursey Belle McCants' judgment on her decision.

"Clara, all I've got to say is, I glory in your spunk."

Clara Atkins finished her morning chores and started dinner for Son. She did not care to eat.

Tears were in her heart — tears that were huge and too terrible to fall from her eyes — tears that backed up and dripped one by one, like raindrops on a tin roof, on a tender spot in her heart.

She finished cooking dinner and sat in her rocker on the front porch to wait for Son.

About two-thirty he unlatched the gate, whistling one of the thousand tunes he seemed to have ready for delivery at the drop of a leaf.

"Son," Clara stood up, "you whistling on a day like this?"

"What's a day like this, Grandma Atkins?"

"There's bad trouble in the land, honey."

"Where?"

"Way over there in what they call the Delta."

"That's way away, Grandma Atkins," he shrugged his shoulders. "It's got nothing to do with us."

"Son, it's got everything to do with us. Didn't they tell you all about it in school? They didn't tell you nothing about how serious this trouble is?"

"No."

"No?"

"No. My teacher told us to write what we did on Labor Day."

"Did you?"

"No."

"Why?"

"It was stupid. She just wanted to yap with her friend in the hall while we wrote that stupid stuff."

"You didn't think the teacher ought to be yapping, as you put it, on something important to the whole world?"

"Oh, phooey on teachers! I want to eat."

"I guess you do, at that. Eating cures everything for some people."

"What's eating you, Grandma Atkins? I'm hungry, so I want to eat. That's all."

"I know that, honey. Try as I might, I can't ram some kind of sense in that cute skull of yours."

"You're mad at me, and I haven't done anything but ask you for dinner, which I don't usually have to do because you have it on the table when I come in."

"You mark my word —"

"Don't mark your word on me, Grandma Atkins, because of what's way off somewhere. I want to eat."

"I'm not too sharp today, but I'll have the food on the table by the time you wash up."

"Gee, thanks."

"Gee, thanks," she mumbled to herself.

She could hear Son whistling a new tune. She realized, then, that he whistled for everything: to ignore people, to soothe anger, to hide fear. He whistled his way in and out of everything.

Son ate his dinner and left the table without saying, "Excuse me." He had whistled his way almost out of the kitchen when Clara called him.

"Come here," she said.

"What I've done now?"

"Nothing but walking along there whistling like you own all of God's creation."

They stared at each other a minute.

"Come on back in here a minute," she ordered.

"Mama, I've done nothing."

"You can 'mama me' to death when you want to get out of something."

"Just tell me what I've done."

"It's mostly for the promise of what you *will* do."

"That's not fair, Mama."

"What is fair? Fair? You do as I say, if you're to stay under my roof another night."

She continued in a rash voice.

"Run out yonder to the little house and attend to your needs."

"I don't have any needs."

"You'd better watch your mouth."

"Now listen," she started again, "when you come from out there, get a drink of water and come on in the dining room, where I'll be."

"Grandma Atkins, I'm old enough to know some things. I don't want to go out 'yonder,' and I don't want any water, and I've done nothing."

"Matters little what you want to do; you're *going* to do as I said. And I mean now."

Son pursed his lips, cupped each ear with a hand and galloped out of the kitchen.

She could hear Son whistling his way to the privy and whistling his way back.

He marched into the dining room and straight to her chair, as her Jim used to do to unnerve her.

"Kneel down," she ordered.

"In the wide-open daylight?"

"You heard what I said."

"I'm eleven."

"I don't care if you're seventy-seven. Come on here to my knees."

Son kneeled down and began trembling with laughter.

"My hind part is sticking out mighty far, Mama."

"Sure. You just shut your impudent mouth."

A tear hit the nape of his neck.

She placed a short, plump hand on each shoulder and patted Son as she used to pat his buttocks to show affection when he was a little fellow.

"This we ask in Thy name. Amen. Now get up." She brushed him away. "Go open the closet."

"Okay."

"Now take this chair and sit it careful over those jars. No," she directed him, "turn the front of the chair to face the wall."

He obeyed her.

"Now you sit in the chair."

"I thought you wanted me to stand up to reach something for you on the high shelf."

"No. You can just as well sit to get at what I want."

Clara shut the closet door and turned the lock as Son sat down.

"Hey, Mama. What's the big idea? It's dark with the door shut. How can I get what you want?"

"What I want is for you to sit yourself in that chair and think until I unlock the door."

"I can't think in this musty place and in the dark like this, Mama."

She heard a thudding, crashing sound in the closet.

"If it was the electric chair, you'd stand it whether you want to or not, Son."

She dusted the furniture in the dining room as Son clamored for attention.

"Mama, mama," he called plaintively.

"Um-hum."

"Mama, I'm dying. I swear the rats are eating me alive."

"Um-hum. Where'd you get that talk?"

"Mama, mama. I'm dying. I cross my heart."

"You'd better not wear yourself out, Son."

"Mama, something's crawling on my neck. Something cold. Oh, Lordy Lord. Mercy, Lord. Mama, it's going to choke me."

"You'd better be quiet. That's your own devilish mind on you. Why don't you whistle?"

"You know I can't see how to whistle in here."

"You're mean, Mama. I didn't know you were so mean. I don't care if you don't ever let me out. I won't have to go to school."

"Well, I'll be about my work then." She felt satisfied now that she knew that something could pierce his middle. He could feel.

She went on to clean the kitchen and then she sorted clothes for the next day's laundry.

On finishing these chores, she unlocked the closet.

She looked at him as if she had never seen him before, when he came out of the closet. He would not face her.

"Son, you all right?" she asked.

"Yes."

"Are you sure?"

"Yes, except I broke something."

She inspected his khaki trousers that were splattered with a reddish mess.

"You broke a quart of strawberry preserves, and I didn't have but two."

"I didn't mean to, honestly, Grandma Atkins."

"If that's all you break before you leave this world, you'll be doing fine." She smiled.

"I'll go clean up. And I swear — I mean, I promise I'll pick you a whole bucket full of strawberries next spring."

"Now I want you to tell me about the closet," she said.

"It was black dark."

"I want you to remember that when you walk the streets of Wedgefield or any other street anywhere."

"Why, Mama?"

"You haven't started feeling, yourself, yet, but you will. When that happens, I don't want you to see nothing but black when it comes to womenfolks."

"Mama, I'm not thinking about girls. That's way off."

"Whether you're thinking about them or not, I mean for you to check on that whistling. Every time you whistle, you just think back and make pretense like you were locked up to not ever get out."

"I swear, Grandma Atkins, if I have to think about your joke every time I whistle, I don't care if I ever whistle again."

"You watch your mouth, Son, when you talk to me."

He sat there kicking at nothing steadily with his right foot.

"You can whistle. That's the way your heart talks. All I want you to do is to make sure your tune don't catch up with the wrong ears."

Dinner Party

The Principal introduced the stranger on the platform as Mr. Joshua Jasper, Jr., President of the Crystal Hill Branch of the CPASNDFMC (Council on the Promotion of Abstinence from the So-Called Negro Diets in the Face of Meticulous Circumstances) and author of the book entitled *The Laws of Freedom.*

Mr. Jasper moved to the left side of the lectern, viewed the packed gymnasium a minute, moved to the right side, then moved in front of it.

"The world is waiting for you!" He drew the index finger of his right hand on the audience as a professional lawman halts his assailant.

Paul Brock rose and stood to attention.

Someone pulled him down to his seat and rebuked him: "He ain't talking to you; he ain't talking to nobody."

"You sick?" the person asked.

He shook his head.

"No needs to get sick on what you hear these day, child. Ain't no world nowhere I know of waiting for no nigger."

Paul finally looked around to see who was prodding him, but all faces were set toward the platform.

"The time is now," Mr. Jasper continued. "Let me repeat for emphasis. *The time is now.* Every Negro must shoulder the burden of the race. Every Negro. And I want every person under the sound of my voice, who can pick up his own feet, or who can pick up his own fork, to make a pledge tonight for the uplifting of our race."

The Principal gave a signal for the audience to rise.

"Now I want all of you to join in the great anthem of freedom as you march to the front. If you don't know the words," Mr. Jasper instructed them, "hum as you march." He left the platform and stood on the bottom step to the stage with a microphone in one hand and an open book in the other. "I want you to place the palm of your right hand on the open book, then place that hand on your heart and keep it there until the procession is over."

They sang, as they marched, "We Shall Overcome." Some mothers carried their arm babies through the ritual and shed tears over their own belief in the future greatness of the race.

When the audience was reseated, Mr. Jasper told them about the pledge which they had taken. "My dears," he smiled, and stroked his goatee, "this is what each one of you have promised: I will not eat foods that are labeled 'Colored' in the presence of members of the other race. These foods are: greens and cornbread, sweet potatoes, pork chops and, above all, watermelon. If I must eat these foods to maintain a nutritional balance under doctor orders, I will eat them in solitude or only in the presence of members of the Negro race. But if I have enough discipline to abstain entirely from these foods labeled 'Colored,' I will have become an honor to my race."

The crowd sang "We Shall Overcome" as they left the meeting — carrying the tune along with them in various paths leading home.

Town talk had it that Wedgefield was hypnotized by the new law. The parents had practically ignored the real reason for the late-August meeting, a discussion of the new Home Economics and Industrial Arts program at the high school. The parents had voted to accept the apprentice plan for seniors in Industrial Arts and home-making practice for the ones in Home Economics. The Principal took it upon himself to coach the sixteen seniors who were to be in carpentry, painting and brickmasonry the first week of school, to be sure that they were brought up to date on practices excluded in the Jasper law.

"And if by any chance," the Principal warned them on the last day, as they prepared to meet their employers for the term, "you bring disgrace to the school or the race by acting like a you-know-what, you'll not get a diploma from Webster High School. As I was saying — oh, here's Mr. Greene now. We're ready to join the men in the shop who'll be your employers."

The sixteen seniors went to the Industrial Arts shop in little-boy clusters. When they entered the shop, they saw a group of middle-aged white men sitting in a row. They ambled toward the opposite side of the room and sat down quietly. Finally Paul started laughing. All of the others laughed with him. Mr. Greene, who was seated behind the visitors, waved silently and frowned. They continued to laugh as Mr. Greene made a wry smile, then clenched his teeth as his heavy jaws quivered. They knew that they were acting like you-know-whats, but they could not stop laughing.

Ignoring the laughter, Mr. Greene cleared his throat and made his short explanation: "Each Friday, boys, the gentlemen will pick you up here at one o'clock and take you to work. After you've completed the work assigned to you at each of your separate places, they'll take you home. Now I will call the name of the gentleman, then one of your names, which means you're the apprentice to that gentleman. I'll ask the gentleman to stand, then I want you to stand so that you can start knowing each other."

Paul's employer, Mr. Hollis Earle, was a tall, friendly looking man with deep-set green eyes and a hooked nose. They looked at each other across the room, neither venturing to smile.

———

The next Friday afternoon, at twelve forty-five, Mr. Earle stepped into the shop. He was searching, undoubtedly, for a boy with some distinguishing feature that would mark himself as his apprentice. After failing to recognize Paul, he said, "Your teacher told me to pick up my boy, whosoever he is."

"That's me," Paul said, and walked over to Mr. Earle.

"Sonny boy, think you'll like it with me?"

"Yes sir," he replied, "long as I lay some bricks."

"We'll lay'm, awright. Don't you so much as worry, we'll lay'm sure's we got hands."

"Yes sir," he replied.

"Now look here, sonny boy, don't you start no flinching and going on, 'cause you'll be just like at home once you get to know Mrs. Earle. Mrs. Earle's a home missionary. You ever get free Christmas at your house?"

"No sir."

"It's a wonder you didn't, but if you did, Mrs. Earle had something to do with it. She said wasn't no needs to go running in the jungle after Africans and all these good Nigrahs right here in Wedgefield'n about a-needing help. Pretty right, eh, sonny boy?"

"Yes sir."

Paul sat beside Mr. Earle, flinching without making violent movements. He pressed his teeth between his tongue, cutting it until he thought he tasted blood. Mr. Earle drove his half-old Ford pick-up truck over and away from the center marking on the highway in a zigzag fashion over the speed limit until they reached a suburban community called Wayside Square. As they began circling blocks, he drove slower and started to talk again.

"Who your folks, sonny boy?"

"Mrs. Sadie Wingate's my daddy's mother off Levey Land —"

"You hush, boy. I was so high"— he took his right hand off the wheel—"when Levey cleared that land."

"My daddy's the one called Melvin Lee, but he's a Brock because Grandma married a Brock when she left Levey Land Plantation."

"Lord, boy, I had my first job clerking in Levey's commissary when Johnny Wingate died and Sadie had to leave Levey Land. And now here you, her grand boy, talking about laying bricks. I tell you it's a good thing to do on rainy days and 'twixt crops."

"Yes sir. But I meant to lay bricks straight out because I didn't want to be no kind of farmer —"

"Here we are." Mr. Earle pulled up in the yard of a sprawling new blond-brick ranch-styled house which had not been land-scaped.

"See, we got a lot to do so's to get to laying bricks a little later on."

"Yes sir," Paul answered.

It was about one-thirty when they reached Mr. Earle's place. Paul walked around the yard and finally went to the patio to sit on a bench. Two red hounds greeted him as he sat alone to wait for orders.

"Say, sonny boy," Mr. Earle appeared with a tray table and sat it down before Paul, "you might as well start out here the right way." He pulled a wad of paper towels from one of his hip pockets and handed it to Paul. "A piece of soap's on the inside. Rinse your hands off there at the faucet and I'll watch your dinner."

He washed his hands and sat down before his dinner: Pork roast, collard greens, cornbread muffins and candied yams. As he sat watching the food, Mr. Earle returned with a pint glass of cold buttermilk.

"I'm going back in, so's you can eat like you want to. Don't pay no mind to Dan o'Shanter and O'Bully."

Paul enjoyed his dinner, emptying the paper plate. He then tantalized the red hounds by fanning the food-scented paper plate across their noses.

For two Fridays he enjoyed meals on the patio that Mrs. Earle sent by her husband. He ate heartily while the red hounds looked on, feeling sure that he was exempt from the Jasper Law because he ate his meals alone.

Mr. Joshua Jasper, Jr., was scheduled to address the WCCCM (Wedgefield Colored Club for Cultural Maneuvers) the last week in September, when they would celebrate their first anniversary. The Principal had been disturbed so often about the Jasper Law that he had decided, in self-defense, to call a meeting at the school so that Mr. Jasper himself could repeat the pledge while he was in Wedgefield. Mr. Jasper consented without a moment of hesitation.

The gymnasium was packed, just as it had been the first night when Mr. Joshua Jasper, Jr., stood to issue what the audience expected to be an earth-shaking, lambasting proclamation on the punishment for lawbreakers after repeating the pledge. He stood before the lectern, however, with both arms hanging at his sides. In a moderate tone he began to talk: "I am not going to repeat the pledge. I will have copies of *The Laws of Freedom* on sale at the end of this program. If you are unable to purchase one tonight in order to read the pledge to yourself — it's on page 34 — I will leave an ample enough supply with your Principal so that you can get one later."

He poured a glass of water, drank it leisurely and then started again: "I have heard about your using the pledge to gain for your own ends. I've heard that some women declare that members of the race should eat only choice beef cuts and fowl. Others say that only meat substitutes should be served. Some claim that the adults may eat whatever they want to, but children under twelve should be held to the pledge. Now, I need not spell it out — but I will. In the first place, these ladies want what they haven't been able to afford. In the second case, they perhaps desire to cheat on necessities to have a few luxuries. In the third instance, they feel that rules are made for children, not adults. And now you want to know what punishments we have to fit your various offenses. None. You will live with the deed and your conscience. This is strictly an honor system. Oh, the other thing I want to say is that the Principal has kindly consented to set up a Junior Branch of CPASNDFMC here at Webster High School. And I thank you for listening."

The crowd went away grumbling and swearing and pledging not to buy a single copy of *The Laws of Freedom*. They would have proven their loyalty by singing heartily even if they could not refrain from eating colored foods. If he had only allowed them to sing "We Shall Overcome," he himself would have felt their sincerity. He had spoiled the glory of it all by not abusing them. He had shown signs of a weak leader by not having suitable punishment meted out for the lawbreakers.

Now he was going to trust the younger generation to laud it over their elders. He had asked to organize a Junior Branch, when no Senior Branch of the CPASNDFMC existed in Wedgefield.

The sad, sad end, that each man had been called upon to discipline himself, was a fault never to be forgiven.

―――――

For the first time Paul felt that he had been called upon individually to support a cause. He was not sure that he understood the laws of freedom, because he had always thought that freedom gave a person the chance to operate without restrictions. The way Mr. Jasper put it the second time gave him the idea that nobody was going to be free. Now he began to realize that he had no right to enjoy his meals alone if he ate the forbidden foods.

When Mr. Earle brought his dinner to him the next Friday, he was relieved to find none of the forbidden food on his plate. Still, he did not enjoy the meal. The thing which worried him the most was whether he could refuse a meal if it were the wrong meal. He made a pledge to himself to go to the lunchroom at eleven o'clock so that he would not need to eat at Mr. Earle's house. If he did not have enough for a plate lunch, he would buy a bag of parched peanuts or candy bars from the vendor to kill his appetite until he could reach home. He would drink only water at the Earles' and if his ribs pinched him, he decided that it was nobody's business but his own.

He was nominated Vice-President of the Junior Branch and felt now that he had to keep the pledge as an act of will not only for himself now, but to encourage the other young people that he would lead.

For once Paul was put out with having to work with Mr. Earle. If he were not working with a Caucasian, he would have no occasion to be in close quarters with a member of the other race. To fortify his resolve, he ate in the lunchroom and bought two candy bars so that hunger would not plague him on the job.

That afternoon they finished cleaning the stack of old bricks which they had been working on since he started his apprenticeship. Just two hours before he was due to leave, Mr. Earle called:

"Come on up and wash your hands, sonny boy."

Paul washed his hands and sat down to rest on the patio. He could hear the conversation going on inside.

"Josie," Mr. Earle said, "you know they like watermelon."

"I'll show them," Paul thought. And somehow he felt that people five blocks away heard his protest.

"Sonny boy," Mr. Earle called him to the door, "come here and get this folding table and open it up on the patio."

"Yes sir," he replied.

For the first time he saw Mrs. Earle. She came out smiling nicely like one of the ladies he had seen in *The Christian Ladies Magazine* that his mother brought from work.

"How you?" she said. "Mr. Earle's been telling me what beautiful work you do to be a high school boy. That's so nice. The school is helping to make you all something worthwhile. And it's so thoughtful for the business men like Mr. Earle to help you all really do something skillful with your hands."

"Yes ma'm," he answered, and didn't know what to do with his eyes, his hands or his feet.

Mr. Earle put a Dixie Queen watermelon on the table and cut it into quarters.

"Come on and get a piece of watermelon, sonny boy."

"Oh, no sir," Paul protested. "Like I said, I had a real big lunch."

"Boy, it's past three o'clock." Mr. Earle plucked a chunk from the heart and munched it with relish. "That lunch's settled."

"No sir, I don't care for any; I'll go on and put the bricks in the truck." He got up to leave.

"Come on, sonny. There's no more'n enough for us all. You know they're really out of season. We were just lucky —"

"No ma'm, really —"

"You going to let your last chance pass by just because you're a little shamefaced. I tell you what," Mr. Earle said, "we'll eat ours and go on in the house so you can enjoy yours all by yourself just like you did before now."

"No, you come on here and sit to this table." Mrs. Earle patted a chair.

Paul remembered that it was bad manners to have a lady begging you to do something that you could do without any trouble. He moved up to the table and cut out a small chunk, which he took to his mouth on the tip of the knife blade.

"Have another piece." Mrs. Earle was cutting the remaining quarter into three slices. "You know this melon's good, sonny boy." She handed him the slice, which he took without wrangling.

As Paul began to feel cool and satisfied as his teeth sank into the slice of melon, the voice of Joshua Jasper, Jr., began to taunt him. "If you just have to eat these forbidden foods, do it with your own color or in strict privacy."

O'Bully and Dan o'Shanter sat on their haunches, catching bits of watermelon which Mrs. Earle threw to them.

"Aren't they cute?" she said. "They'll eat anything we eat."

"Yes ma'm," Paul agreed, and talked to the hounds and fed them bits of his watermelon.

That evening Paul asked to walk home. He was half-tickled and half-alarmed by the afternoon experience. Mrs. Earle had been kind, so he had to use good manners. Watermelon was practically out of season, and he liked it very much, but in the final analysis, he had broken the law. He had become a leader who forsook his own cause. He decided that he needed an adult counselor who could help him to make suggestions that might help him to make positive decisions in the face of such encounters.

At first he thought of his parents, but he soon dismissed them. His father would say, "Don't you ever act like a you-know-what, no matter how you pressed to the wall." And his mother would have given her final answer to the question of life: "Life is an unplanned trip even when you have a ticket in your hand and know the train you're going to catch and the number of your seat."

This time he wanted a new-made answer to his new problem.

Tickle Britches — he was the man to see. He knew everything and everybody. As Wedgefield's man of the world — who sold peanuts on Gregg's Corner when he wasn't assisting the school men, lawyers, doctors, widows or morticians — he shared his wisdom with white and black, young and old.

Paul decided to shock him by playing up his flaunting of the Jasper Law when he was a chosen leader for the young Negroes in Wedgefield.

"Hey there." He didn't have even a nickel to buy a bag of peanuts for a sham. "Boys, I'm in a fix. Feel here, my stomach's like a drum. I ruined those Earles by killing a half Dixie Queen."

"You don't say, you don't say, 'n' Jack Frost almost here."

'Yeah, had it with the Earles on their patio — you know, over there in Wayside Square."

"Boy," he pursed his purplish lips, "you're not going up there to that school to learn to be a fool, eh?"

"No sir," Paul answered.

"You're smart boy, enjoying yourself like that. I tell you, you already learned what some of them men up there in Washington won't never learn: don't let your right hand know what the left hand do. The F.B.I. fellow know how to do it, though."

"What're you really saying, Tickle?"

"I'll tell you what was told to me about some 'nother preacher and how he did with a rule 'most like the Jasper Law, and you can get what you can out of it."

"Go ahead." Paul sat on the bench beside Tickle Britches and listened.

"See, this preacher thought like Jasper that colored folks could bring honor to themselves and the race on account of not eating the same stuff they talking 'bout now. Only they had the best a-tall in that law — chitt'lins. Anywise, he preached on this every Sunday. When he went home to dinner with the members, he'd eat a respectable 'tater custard, but if there was any baked ones, he'd tell them to wrap'm up for his friend. Say, if a member had ham, chicken 'n' pork chops, he'd eat chicken on account of it being the preacher-diet, but he'd ask them to wrap the ham and pork chops up for his friend. See, the ham was pork before it was cured."

"But wasn't his best friend colored, too? Wasn't he going against the cause just the same?" Paul asked.

"That's the way my brother reasoned when he heard it. He got nerve enough one day to ask the preacher who was supposed to be the one. 'Reverend,' he says, 'don't you think a man's harming his brother and the race if he pass on to a friend all the degradated diet of the law?' The preached asked, 'Who's a man's best friend?' My brother says, 'Hisself, Reverend, to be sure, hisself.' And the preacher says, 'You wrong brother, a man's best friend's his dog.'

"Now you understand, boy?" Tickle was pleased with his own story.

"Sure, Tickle — sure — only you're my best friend." He smiled down on the basket of peanuts.

Tickle gave Paul a hearty handshake and a free bag of parched peanuts.

Mr. Earle started talking about food as soon as he started the truck the next Friday.

"You know, Mrs. Earle worries a whole lot because you don't eat."

"I eat when I'm hungry," Paul answered.

"I'm not so sure, because Mrs. Earle had to coax you a lot to get you to eat that watermelon."

"I wanted to get on to putting the bricks in the truck after I cooled off, and I wasn't hungry anyway. You see, watermelon isn't something that a person has to have."

"And that's just what I'm trying to tell you, boy. The madam has been racking her brains trying to find out why a big, healthy one like you don't want to eat."

"She needn't worry herself," Paul raised his voice louder than he intended to.

"Don't worry, you won't get by the madam." He smiled with satisfaction. "She says schoolboys are hungry all the time, so they need substantial food. When she says lunch, she's not talking about a scad of doll-baby food, like some women. You know, that little play stuff they love to nibble at in those lady club meetings. She means real filling 'twixt the ribs."

"I hope you'll tell her not to bother," he replied, "because I just don't care to eat any more when I come here to work, because I eat lunch at school and don't want nothing else."

"You don't have to try to fool me, sonny. When I was a boy your age, I was always hungry."

Paul smiled, knowing now what he would have to do.

"Get out, boy, and make yourself at home until I get straight. It's such a nice day, and so pleasant here on the patio. Best to enjoy it before old Jack Frost lights on us. Just hold tight for a minute. I'll be right back."

Paul answered with a smile and sat down on the bench. Mrs. Earle came out, moved a plant from the center of the table and spread a plastic party tablecloth on the table.

"Pull up a chair," she requested.

"Yes ma'm." He obeyed.

Mr. Earle returned with a plate of steaming spaghetti and meatballs and creamed potatoes.

"Smells good, huh, boy?"

"Yes sir, sure does." He bowed his head to bless the food.

"I'll be back in a minute."

As soon as Mr. Earle left, O'Bully and Dan o'Shanter eased up under the table.

"Get away," Mr. Earle commanded, shooing the red hounds away. He gave Paul a pint of pink lemonade and piping-hot buttered rolls in a linen napkin. He reached into his hip pocket and handed Paul the silver, rolled neatly in another white linen napkin.

As soon as Mr. Earle left, the hounds returned. O'Bully sat on his haunches beating a rhythmic staccato with his tail. Dan o'Shanter stretched out, front paws forward, opening and closing his eyes to subdue his longing.

When Paul unwrapped the butter-soaked rolls, Dan o'Shanter lost his composure and began crying. He came closer; O'Bully followed.

Paul watched them a minute, then patted each one on the head.

"Welcome, my friends, to this my dinner party. Cry no more, for you shall be served pronto!" Paul stood up and began dividing the food. He dropped two rolls each, some distance apart, for the dogs. He then tore the plate of spaghetti and potatoes carefully in half and set a portion down for each of his guests. He sat then and drank the pint of lemonade.

Paul was still standing, gloating over the success of his dinner party, when Mr. Earle cleared his throat.

"Look here," Mr. Earle said, "you don't expect to play a damn host all day, when we got a load of bricks to lay, do you bub?"

"Oh, no sir." Paul picked up the empty half plates.

They walked on toward the truck, their footsteps sounding on the cement drive. Finally Mr. Earle spoke: "Look here, sonny, I know you're a young fool, and fool you will be. I see that now as clear as day. And that's all right with me, too. But there's something I'm bound to ask you to do."

"Yes sir," Paul listened attentively.

"First chance you get, I want you to tell Mrs. Josie how nice that dinner was, because she made it especially for you."

"Yes sir," Paul replied. "I'll be sure to tell her the first chance I get."

A Ceremony of Innocence

The thick evergreens screened Georgia Ann McCullum's front porch so well that Tisha did not see her sitting in the porch swing until she reached the top step — the eighth, because she had once measured her age by these steps. She had practiced the salutation "Mother" Georgia to pay honor to this distant cousin who had reached the highest point of distinction for a woman in Chute Bay. She had been made the "mother" of Chute Bay Memorial Baptist Church, which had been built by the people in the Bay on a pay-as-you-go basis during the Depression years.

Tisha stood quietly hugging herself in a full-length Natural Emba Autumn Haze mink coat as she waited for the old woman to recognize her. Even though it was a bright day, the temperature held at 23 degrees above zero and a stiff breeze blew in from the north.

The noise of a truck coming down Bay Road jostled the swinger from an apparent reverie. She slipped from the swing and started forward, then recognized Tisha. Their eyes met and held long enough for the old woman to make a good guess. She fumbled in her mind and grunted, then, caught by pain, she backed back to the swing to steady herself. The swing moved backward, almost causing her to miss her seat.

Tisha rushed to clasp her in a bear hug.

"Don't fall, Mother Georgia — please don't fall," she pleaded.

"Don't tell me," Mother Georgia said, "you Flora Dee's baby. Ain't you, now?"

"Yes, Mother Georgia," she answered, and relaxed her grip, helping the old woman to seat herself in the swing.

"This here Tisha. Sweet little Tisha. Just as pretty, too. You look good enough to eat. Your grandpa still call you his 'little spicy gal'?"

"Grandpa hasn't come close to me since I've been home, Mother Georgia."

"That's your own doings. But thang God. Thang God. Thang God. I talk to Him the other night 'bout you, and here He done sent you already. I ain't scared of you just 'cause you gone astray." She cradled Tisha in her arms and nuzzled her thin cheeks with a bottom lip packed hard with Railroad Mill snuff. Coins hit the porch and began to roll as they reeled in this odd pantomine of genuine affection. She finally held Tisha away at arm's length and gloating over her, told of the wonders that had come with the title "Mother" Georgia.

Old white men whose shirts she had ironed until arthritis twisted both of her wrists — who had brought shirts to her even though a one-day service laundry had opened in Crystal Hill — who brought handouts to supplement the $54.00 a month from the "government"— even they used the title of honor "Mother" Georgia, when they had for decades called her "Aunty."

After this rehearsal, Tisha began to pick up the coins from the floor. She found several nickels and a dime, but Mother Georgia, said that that was not all.

"Don't bother yourself," she told Tisha, "go on in and make yourself at home. You needn' act like company, when this your second home. I'm slow but I'm coming."

Tisha walked into the front room, a room she knew by heart before she left Chute Bay. She glanced about, noticing that it was the same. She waited a minute for Mother Georgia, then brushed the bottom of a chair with her fingers to test it for dust. Her fingertips were black with coal dust. She walked to the door to check on the old woman's delay. She did not want to be caught cleaning the chair. She walked to the door and looked out in time to see Mother Georgia crawling about slowly on her knees and fumbling up and down the porch planks with her drawn hands.

"Mother Georgia, can I help —?"

"No, Sugar, I got all but two pennies. Hope the Lord them

two didn't roll off the porch. If it was Mr. Pogue' truck, I'd get my coal if I was a few cents short. But this truck want every cent. I don't know who it b'longt to."

"Come on in, Mother Georgia," Tisha said. "I'll give you what you need for the coal man." She then went out and helped her up from the floor.

"Sugar, they got them ole engines what pull theirself. If they was still using coal like they used to, I'd be out there up and down them tracks with my bucket, picking me up all the coal I want."

"Yes ma'm," Tisha replied. "Now tell me how much the coal cost, and I'll sit out there and wait for the truck."

"No, Sugar. You so dressed up, he might not stop if he don't see me. You just sit tight, and soons he come I'm going to make up a great big fire in the heater. It ain't cold, is it? I got on plenty clothes, and you got on that big fine coat. Don't get hetted up 'cause I got to ask you for myself 'bout that Allie what Flora worried to death 'bout. She worried plumb stiff 'bout that God've yours, just like she can't put you back in your place. Humph. I said send her to me when she come home. I'll get her straight before she go back out yonder."

Tisha pat her feet as Mother Georgia talked, because her toes were getting stiff from cold. A minute later a truck pulled up, and she let Tisha give the driver $1.25 for a crocker sack of coal and a bunch of lightwood splinters. She built a fire in the heater with two splinters and a few lumps of coal. She washed her hands in a basin on the washstand, then sat down to watch Tisha.

"Lord, Sugar, you look good enough to bite on the jaw. The only thing got me bothered is what your ma told me 'bout that Allie. You know you got her nearly distracted? What's that, any-how, child — talking 'bout goin'ta serve Allie? That ain't no God. You know Mother Georgia ain't goin'ta tell you nothing wrong 'long's I had my hand on the gospel plough. That was 'fore they spanked your ma, so you know I'm a soldier. You got no business turning your back on God."

"Allah, Mother Georgia, is the true God. You see, I know He's the right God because of what He's done for me. Okay?" Tisha started to stand, but the old woman waved her back to her chair. "He helps us to have heaven right here on earth, and that's what I want because I can enjoy life every day of my life."

"What I'm telling you—that is, what Mother Georgia, ambassador to Christ, is telling you, is that ain't no God you found up the road. Your ma learned you 'bout the right God from your cradle, and it ought to be good enough to take you to your grave. You see what He's done for me, don't you, child? That Allie you heard tell of way out yonder is just a make-shift God the crowd hark'ning after. And I'm trying to tell you better 'cause, you, Flora and every child she got rest close to my heart. We kin as cousins, but I been a mother to her and to y'all before I come a mother to the church. You better turn to the true and living God 'fore it's a day and hour and eternity too late."

Tisha started to let the argument rest, but she felt that she would be a shameful volunteer for Allah if she let this occasion pass without sharing her idea of his worth.

"I'm serving Allah," she persisted, "and I hope to serve Him better. I'm twenty-two now, and I hope to be that many times stronger in His grace before I'm twice that old."

"I'm going on these here knees, little Miss, to the Master I know who'll open your eyes. Look at me." Mother Georgia hoisted her huge frame from the rocker and fastened her sharp bird eyes on Tisha. "I'm seventy-six-odd years old. How you reckon I make it without the Lord? You see that sack of coal? The Lord sent it here. Let me tell you, the Pastor—I reckon you don't know Reverend Sarks—anyway, he come here faithful as the days is long and brings me ration just like he take it home.

And Mr. Dwyer — I guess you forgot him — he sends me all the bones from his store to feed these six dogs I got on the yard for company. Some of them oxtails 'n stuff the dogs don't see 'cause I make me a pot've soup."

"Well, let's not get excited," Tisha said. I brought a present for you. Let's look after that." Tisha handed her a small Christmas-wrapped package which the old woman shook.

"What these? Drawers?" she asked.

Tisha shook her head. "You see," she told Mother Georgia, "we don't have Christmas, but you do."

"You mean Allie don't let y'all have no Christmas? How do you do when you don't ever have no Christmas? How can you live with no Christmas?"

"Everyday ought to be important in this life." Tisha had lost her ardor.

"Oh, these them pretty head rags? Well, I'm going to wear this cotton one to Prayer Meeting and the silk one on Communion Sunday." She rewrapped the gift in the same paper.

"That will be nice." Tisha was pleased with her happiness over the small gift. It was one of the things she always cherished about Mother Georgia.

It was warm enough now for Tisha to remove her coat. The old woman got up to leave for the kitchen, but Tisha tried to persuade her to relax or, if she insisted on making coffee, to make it on the heater, but she would not listen.

"You're company now," she maintained, "and a fine lady at that, so I'll treat you like one, no matter if you did used to help me out. You make yourself at home now while I get straight in the kitchen. And you get up and turn that coat insadouter so's no smoke'll hit it."

"Yes ma'm," she answered.

———

Tisha sat there remembering the room as she had known it

years before. This room was full of furniture. There was an upright grand piano, a three-piece bedroom suite, a washstand, two rocking chairs, and a davenport with sugar-starched crocheted pieces on the arm rests. The center table held a large metal oil lamp on the top and a big family bible on the bottom tier. The old green wool rug was practically eaten away from the floor, and the wallpaper of unidentified color was smoky and filled with rainwater circles.

There was an array of several pretty vases on the mantlepiece, of odd shapes and sizes, and pictures hung undiscriminately wherever a nail could be placed to hold them. High above the mantle was a picture of Cupid asleep, with the bow and arrow besides him. Glancing around the wall, she found the pictures of undertakers, ministers, church groups, family members, movie stars and flowers. There was a lone insurance policy hanging above the doorsill going to the middle room. She tried to evaluate the holdings of this room in terms of financial worth — the most valuable possessions in the house secured from a lifetime of satisfactory labor. They hardly added up to dollars and cents.

After a while Mother Georgia came in with a cup of coffee and a plate of cake on a tray.

"I made your coffee on the hot plate. I got 'lectric, you know," and she pointed to the bulb hanging on a suspended wire in the center of the room. "I have my lamp lighted half the time before I remember I can pull that little chain to get some light." She watched Tisha a minute, then encouraged her to eat the five slices of cake because she had baked the cakes herself. They were her specials: raisin, chocolate, pineapple, coconut and strawberry jelly.

"Mother Georgia," she said, "you remember the time I ate a whole plateful of cake when I was a child? Well, it was the best cake I'd ever had in my life at that time. And since then I've found out how to enjoy life the way I enjoyed that first plate of cake you gave me. As long as you enjoy this life, there's nothing to worry about."

"I don't want to spoil your appetite, but you're gone from your raising. You're caught in the web of sin. And you know what that mean. You sitting there all pretty, but you dying, Sugar." The old woman shook her head.

Dying! Tisha turned and looked at Georgia Ann McCullum. *She* was dying. The old woman was dying — dying as she had done every day of her life, though she was too good a minstrel man to know it. Her ugly life was death. She no doubt would have a beautiful funeral according to their pattern, with a nice long obituary, good remarks from the deacons, a wailing eulogy from the preacher and honest tears from unknown visitors at the grave; but her life was, and always had been, an ugly death.

"Thang God you come through, Sugar. Look — put your cake you left in a bag and take it home with you. And when you go back up the road, you'll remember what God has done for me and you'll forget about that Allie and the Mooselims. They'll run the world off the map if you not careful. You were raised to know that no colored folks can't rule the world by theirself. My folks told me white folks is a mess, but a nigger ain't nothing."

"Yes ma'm," Tisha said as she put on her coat to leave. She was not going to argue with the old lady because, more than anyone else, Mother Georgia had given her the final proof that she had chosen the right path — the path away from the religion of the Cross. God, the God of Mother Georgia, the God of her parents, the God who had let His only Son be crucified by wicked men, was uncaring. Then, as now, she told herself, if He was up there, He was oblivious of all the Georgia Ann McCullums in the universe.

She pulled the mink closer to her ears as she faced the cold, crisp air on the walk to her parents' home down Bay Road, happy in the thought that she had learned to praise Allah, who cared for His black children enough to help them find heaven on earth.